VISUAL APPROACH SERIES

CW00531505

Chord Construction:
Learning Through Shapes and Forms

By Carol Hawn and Dorothy Munz

ISBN 0-7935-6169-8

HAL•LEONARD® CORPORATION

7777 W. BLUEMOUND RD. P.O. BOX 13819 MILWAUKEE, WI 53213

You, THE USER, can select the learning path.

You may use the pages in the sequence given or in a different order.
The flow chart shown here should help you choose the order that is best for you.
For further information, see How to Use This Book, page 4.

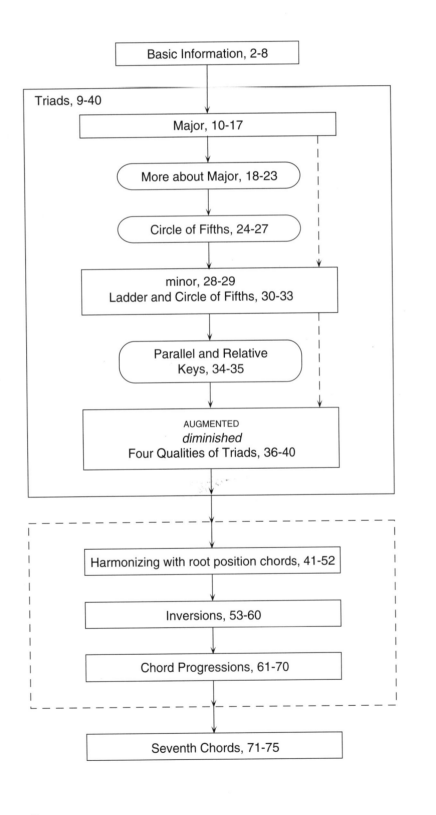

Boxes with sharp corners mean that the material is too important to skip.

Boxes with rounded corners tell you the sequence is optional: Now or later

For example, you may go directly from Major triads, ending on page 17, to minor triads, pages 28-29.

You may prefer to move back and forth between the Triad section and the other parts of the book: for example, from Major triads directly to the chord progressions on page 64, and back again.

You may wish to rearrange the sequence of these sections.

TABLE OF CONTENTS

Arrangements and adaptations in this book are by the authors.

How to Use This Book

This book has been carefully organized to be flexible
so you can use every page in the order given or bypass
a section and come back later. These features can help
you decide how you will want to use the book:

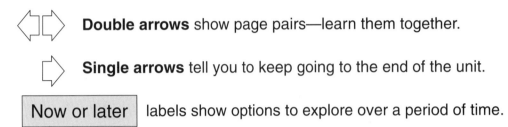

Double arrows show page pairs—learn them together.

Single arrows tell you to keep going to the end of the unit.

Now or later labels show options to explore over a period of time.

The **flow chart** on page 2 helps you see learning paths.

The **Find It Fast** index on page 76 lists the subjects you are looking for.

The book is designed so you can see the big picture (for example, all 15 Major triads are
presented on page 15), but everything on the page does not have to be done all at once.
Select what you want. As another example, on pages 24 and 25 you might work with
the ideas across the top of both pages and then come back for the other two-thirds later.

On some pages the information is **grouped vertically as well as horizontally.** For example,
on page 64 you might explore "PREPARE" in several keys until you are ready for "PLAN." Then
select one of the chord progressions in "PLAN." Work with it in combination with the notation in
"PLAY" or just by itself as finger-movement lines that can be played in any key. Learning the music
notation for the chord progression in several keys is yet another possibility. When you are ready, go
through the same process with the other chord progression. You may return to the index card later.

How to begin with this book:

- Start at pages 6-7 before or after you have begun to read music notation.
- You can use the 5-finger pattern maps (page 77) right away, before you read notation,
  along with the keyboards on pages 13 and 15. These keyboards also facilitate
  transposing music on the facing pages.
- Come back to page 8 as often as you want, to work with triads and letter names.
- Pages 10-17 are the first learning unit.
  See the big picture on a page, then select parts to learn during the week (pages 14-15).
- Expand with options on pages 18-27, or go directly to minor triads on pages 28-29.
- At this point, look at the flow chart to see where you will go next:
  continue through the triad section?
  on page 64 learn one of the chord progressions with finger-movement lines?
  harmonize melodies (pages 42-49)?
  play inversions?

Page 5 shows you the visuals that will help you SEE what you FEEL and HEAR.
Be sure to take the **Lift-Outs** with you to other music you are playing!

TOOLS for Success in Learning Chords

Lift-Outs
shape your hand.

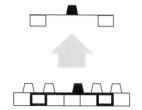

They are lifted out of
the keyboard profile to represent
either Major or minor chords.

This example shows
a D Major triad.

Interval-Width Notation
shows you the difference
between half steps
and whole steps.

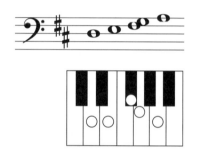

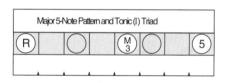

Major 5-Note Pattern and Tonic (I) Triad

On the staff, notes that touch
show half steps.

On the keyboard, circles that
almost touch show half steps.

On the Movable Keyboard Maps,
circles that almost touch
show half steps.

White circles on
Movable Keyboard Maps
show you where to put your fingers.

Slide the maps to start
from any black or white key.

Use them in combination
with Lift-Outs.

Cut them out from the back
of the book. Fasten to card stock
if you wish.

From one square to the next
is a half step. The small triangles
at the bottom line up with the
cracks between the keys.

Keyboard and Staff Relationships

Keyboard letter names

  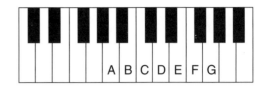

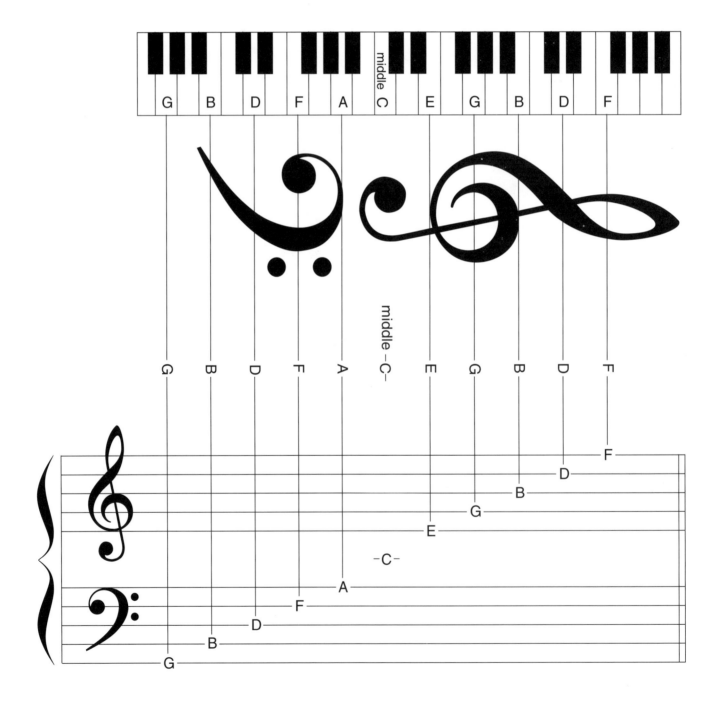

Keyboard and Staff Relationships (continued)

Beethoven, "Ode to Joy" from the Ninth Symphony.

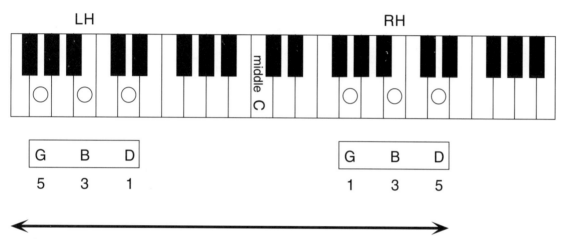

Your hands FEEL chords on the keyboard horizontally.

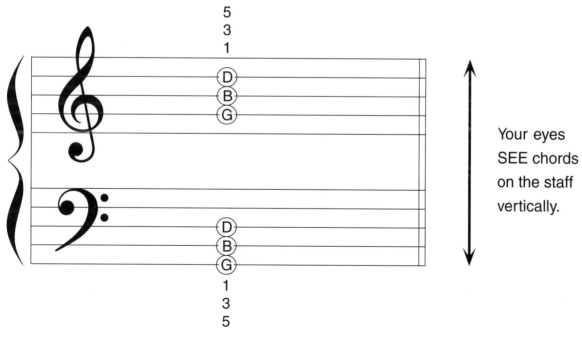

Your eyes SEE chords on the staff vertically.

Some Basic Information about Chords

A chord with three notes is called a TRIAD. In music notation,
a root position triad has three notes that touch. It can be
written on lines or in spaces.

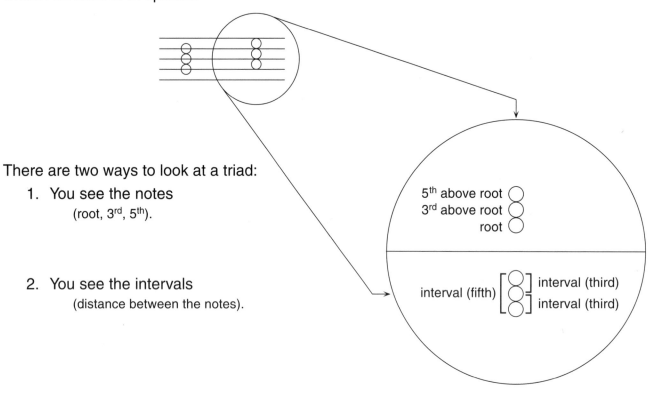

There are two ways to look at a triad:

1. You see the notes
    (root, 3rd, 5th).

2. You see the intervals
    (distance between the notes).

Triads have seven letter names.
Play the seven rectangles below.

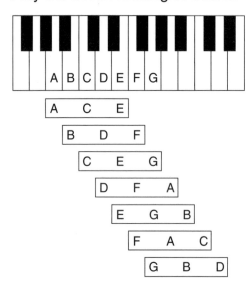

PREVIEW

There are four qualities (sizes) of triads.
Play the keyboards and HEAR the difference.

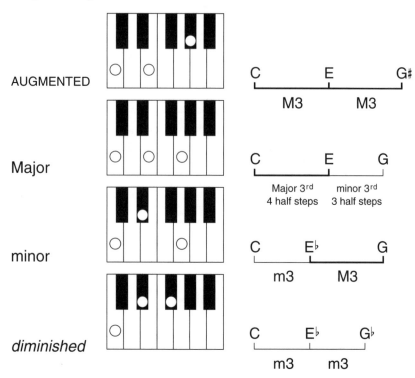

TRIADS

- Build **Major** triads

    from the first 5 scale degrees
    from intervals

    Choose ways to review them

    Accompany a song

- Build **minor** triads

    from the first 5 scale degrees
    from intervals
    from parallel Major triads

    Explore summaries

    Play triad arpeggio patterns

- Build **AUGMENTED** and ***diminished*** triads

    Choose ways to play them

LEARN Chords Faster by Understanding Whole and Half Steps and Scales

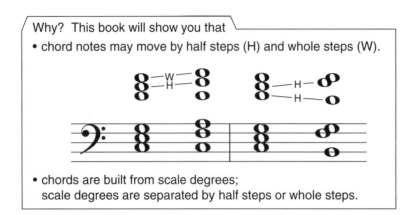

Why? This book will show you that
- chord notes may move by half steps (H) and whole steps (W).

- chords are built from scale degrees;
  scale degrees are separated by half steps or whole steps.

HEAR the difference

Half steps: Play pairs of notes: there is no key between fingers.

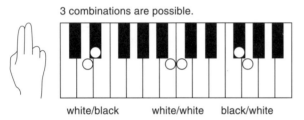

3 combinations are possible.

white/black   white/white   black/white

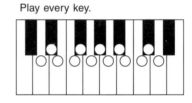

Play every key.

Whole steps: Play pairs of notes: there is a key between fingers.

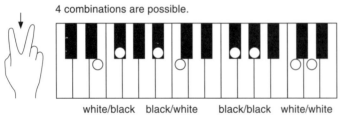

4 combinations are possible.

white/black   black/white   black/black   white/white

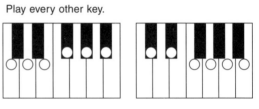

Play every other key.

SEE the Major scale pattern

	whole and half steps	W		W	H	W		W		W	H
	fingerprints	○		○	○○		○		○		○○
	scale degrees	1		2	3 4		5		6		7 8
											(1)

You will be using the first 5 notes of this pattern to build Major chords.

LEARN Major chords in the first 5 notes of Major scales

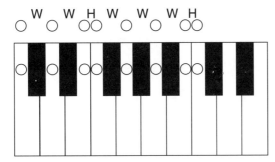

FEEL the Major scale pattern on the keyboard

Place your fingers (no thumbs) on all the white keys from **C** to **C**.
Now slide your fingers into the narrow part of the keys near the fallboard.
You feel black keys between your fingers where the whole steps are.

SEE the Major scale pattern in notation

FIND a Major triad in the first 5 notes of the scale

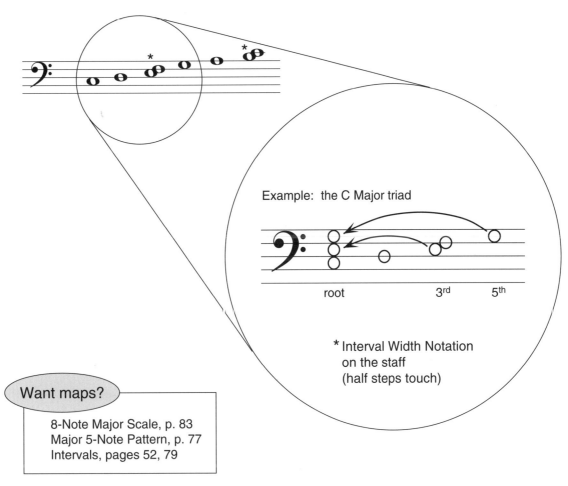

Example: the C Major triad

root   3rd   5th

* Interval Width Notation
on the staff
(half steps touch)

Want maps?

8-Note Major Scale, p. 83
Major 5-Note Pattern, p. 77
Intervals, pages 52, 79

PLAY the white circles (finger-prints)

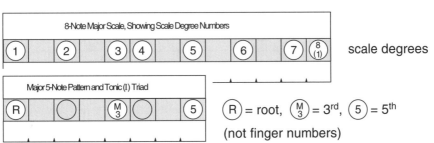

8-Note Major Scale, Showing Scale Degree Numbers

| 1 | 2 | 3 | 4 | 5 | 6 | 7 | 8 (1) |

scale degrees

Major 5-Note Pattern and Tonic (I) Triad

| R | | M3 | | 5 |

$\left(R\right)$ = root, $\left(\begin{smallmatrix}M\\3\end{smallmatrix}\right)$ = 3rd, $\left(5\right)$ = 5th

(not finger numbers)

To begin these patterns anywhere on the keyboard, slide the maps you have cut out.

Triads

LEARN 5-Note Major Patterns

Once you know all twelve 5-Note Major patterns,
all you have to do is play bottom/middle/top (root, 3rd, 5th)
of each one to put every Major triad into your hands.

5-Note Major Pattern   in an 8-Note Major Scale

Where you FIND them

12 places: on five black keys
and seven white keys

} as shown on the next page.

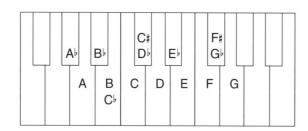

NOTE

There are 15 Major scales and 15
Major triads, because three of them
have two letter names. These are
called Enharmonic Keys (same
sound, different notation).

Want a map?

Hands separately: Use the Major 5-Note Pattern Map.   } page 77
Hands together: Use the One Octave Apart Map.

What you PLAY

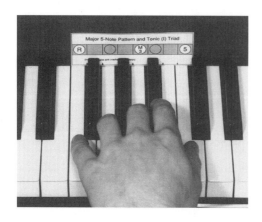

Play this melody on each keyboard on the next page
to transpose it into all 15 Major keys.

PLAY 5-Note Major Patterns in Four Groups

NOTE
Circles show the pattern, not exact finger placement.

Use these patterns to play the melody on page 12.
They are grouped by shape to make them easier to learn.

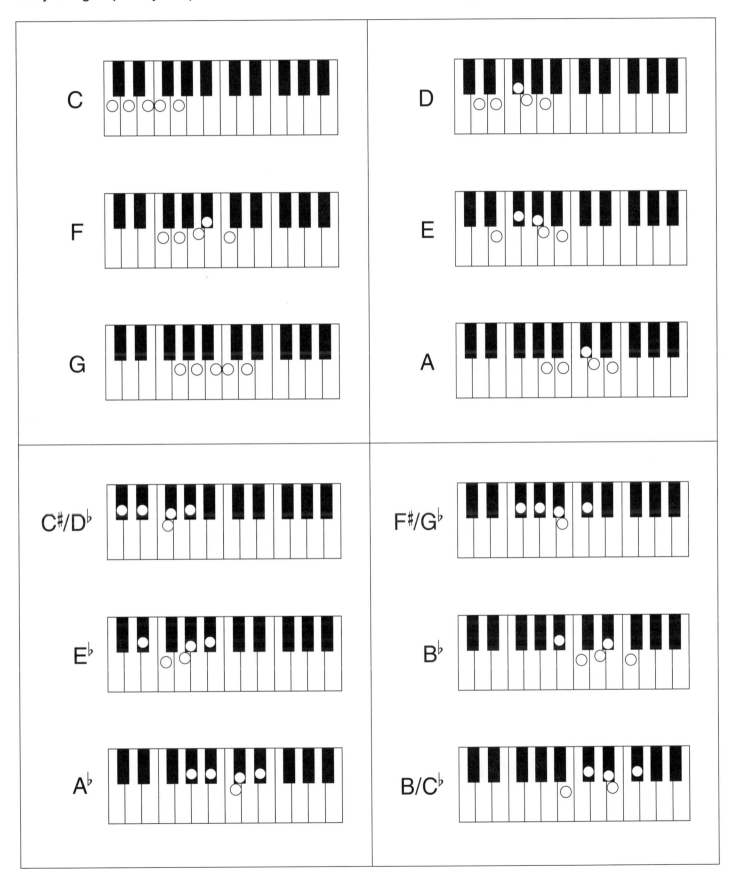

Triads

BUILD Major Triads with

Bottom	Middle	Top
Root	**3rd**	**5th**

of a 5-Note Major Pattern

The root is the letter name of the chord.
Example: D Major.

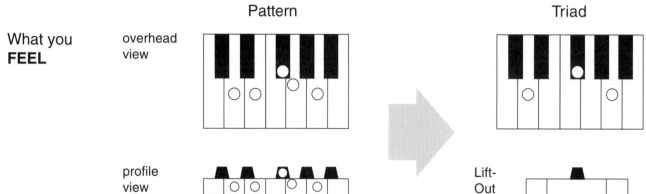

Pattern   Triad

What you FEEL

overhead view

profile view

Lift-Out

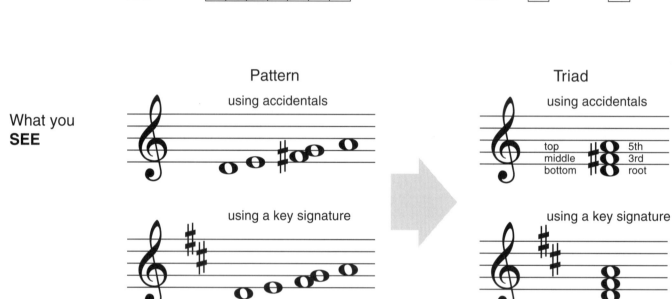

Pattern   Triad

What you SEE

using accidentals

using a key signature

using accidentals

top   5th
middle   3rd
bottom   root

using a key signature

What you PLAY

Play this pattern
of steps and skips
on each keyboard
on the next page.

Map Help, p. 77

hands separately: Major 5-Note Pattern
hands together: Major 5-Note Patterns
                  One Octave Apart

Triads

PLAY All 15 Major Triads Grouped by Lift-Out Shape So They Are Easy to Learn

1. Play the fingerprints on the keyboards one at a time like a melody;
   then play them together like the chord written on the staff.

2. Play the melody on page 14 on each of these keyboards.

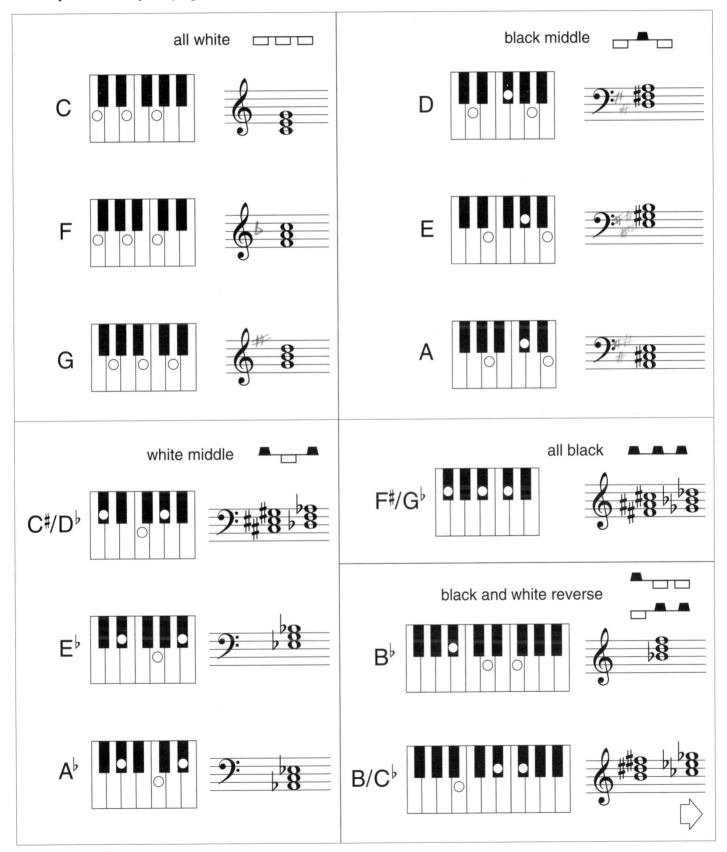

How Do You Know Whether to Use Sharps or Flats When You Spell Scales and Chords?

Now or later

B C♯ ? ? ?   B♭ C ? ? ?

Answer: 1. Keep the letters in alphabetic order:

ABCDE   BCDEF   CDEFG   DEFGA   EFGAB   FGABC   GABCD

2. Add the accidentals that will keep the pattern of whole and half steps.

Here is how to spell the examples above:

1 Play the pattern:

2 Think of the alphabet.

5-Note Pattern   Chord

3 Write the letters of the alphabet. Add sharps or flats to keep the pattern of whole and half steps.

B

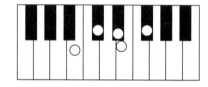

BCDEF

B   C♯   D♯   E   F♯

B♭

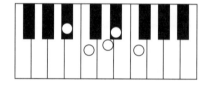

BCDEF

B♭   C   D   E♭   F

In B Major and B♭ Major the notes are written the same; the key signatures change the pitches. Chord letter names are shown. Use the Lift-Outs to help find the correct keys. (Adapted from Offenbach's "Cancan.")

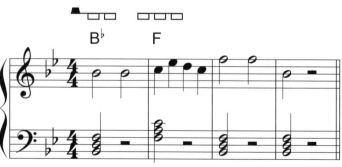

16

Triads

BUILD Major Triads with Intervals

An interval is the distance between two notes.

What you THINK

Play the D Major triad, DF♯A, below, which uses scale degrees 1, 3, 5.
Now focus on the distance between the scale degrees.

> **The alphabet identifies the intervals as thirds.**
> D to F, (DEF, three letter names)

> **The number of half steps tells you what kind of thirds they are.**

from one key to the next key is a half step

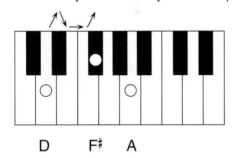

D   F♯   A

from one square to the next square is a half step

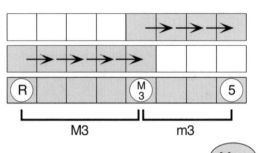

Map — See page 77.

What you FEEL

Major triads are built by stacking up two thirds.
The bottom third has 4 half steps and the top third has 3 half steps.

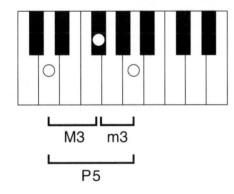

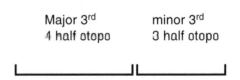

Major 3ʳᵈ   minor 3ʳᵈ
4 half steps   3 half steps

What you SEE

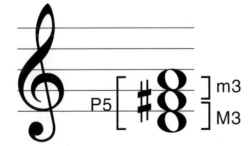

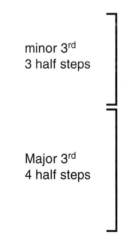

minor 3ʳᵈ
3 half steps

Major 3ʳᵈ
4 half steps

PLAY Major Triads Grouped as Opposite Lift-Outs

Now or later

Another way to play is sliding the Movable Keyboard Map by half steps—
from D♭ to D, E♭ to E takes you through opposite Lift-Out shapes.

In this book chord letter names are often placed under the staff, closest to the root.
Lead sheet notation places letter names above the staff.

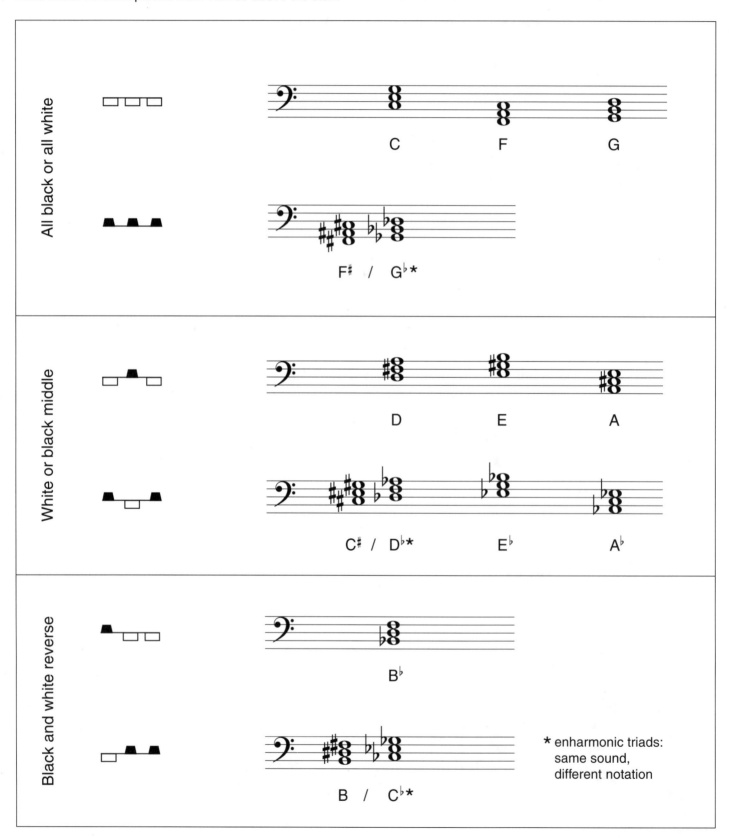

All black or all white

C   F   G

F# / G♭*

White or black middle

D   E   A

C# / D♭*   E♭   A♭

Black and white reverse

B♭

B / C♭*

* enharmonic triads:
  same sound,
  different notation

Triads

PLAY Major Triads as Broken Chords (Arpeggios)

Now or later

When you are ready for variety,

    play them top to bottom instead of bottom to top,
    use pedal,
    and change the rhythm.

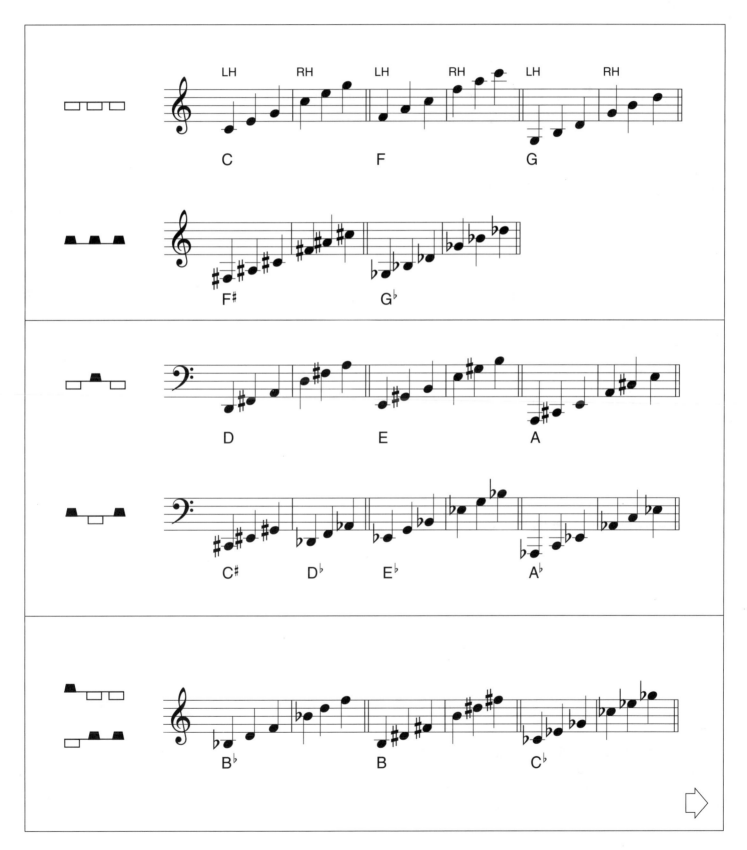

DEVELOP Confidence and Facility Playing Arpeggios (Broken Chords)

Now or later

The two arpeggio patterns on these facing pages will
enable you to play all over the keyboard in many keys.

Look at page 19 again. Notice that it presents
a two-measure broken chord in every Major key.

Arpeggio Pattern #1 begins with the two-measure broken chord pattern
from page 19, repeats it, then repeats it again and adds roots to bring it to a conclusion.

Play the pattern, using a black-middle Lift-Out ( ) on A .

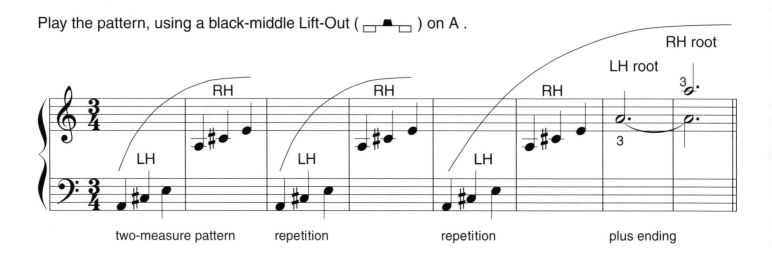

Now mentally remove all the staff lines and notation and just think of the pattern
you played. It would look like this:

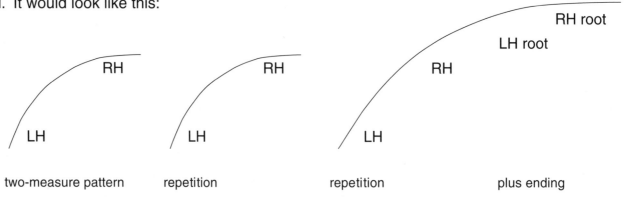

Turn back to page 19, choose another Lift-Out and key, and watch the pattern above as you play it
again. See how easy it would be to play it with any of those Lift-Outs and keys on page 19?

In musical terms, this is known as transposing to another key.

Triads

EXPAND Your Playing Ability with Arpeggios

Now or later

Arpeggios work well as accompaniments and fill-ins.

Arpeggio Pattern #2 is fun to play because it goes up and down almost the entire keyboard. It is easy because one hand plays the notes the other hand just played.

Figure out your "moves" from the notation below. This example uses an all-white Lift-Out (⬜⬜⬜) in the key of C Major. Try other keys, too.

TIP

Just count the number of LH/RHs (there are 4 of them—try it out in the air first) and cross over with the root.

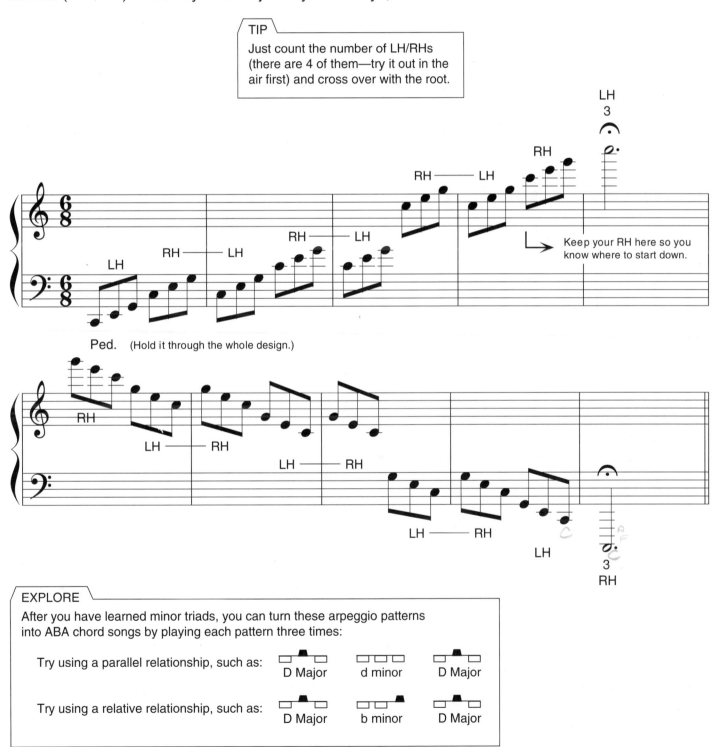

Keep your RH here so you know where to start down.

Ped.   (Hold it through the whole design.)

EXPLORE

After you have learned minor triads, you can turn these arpeggio patterns into ABA chord songs by playing each pattern three times:

Try using a parallel relationship, such as: D Major   d minor   D Major

Try using a relative relationship, such as: D Major   b minor   D Major

ENJOY This Song Applying What You Have Learned

It's easy to start with the chord group C, F and G.

All white: □□□

Joyfully: "Oh, when the saints go marching in" (traditional American song).

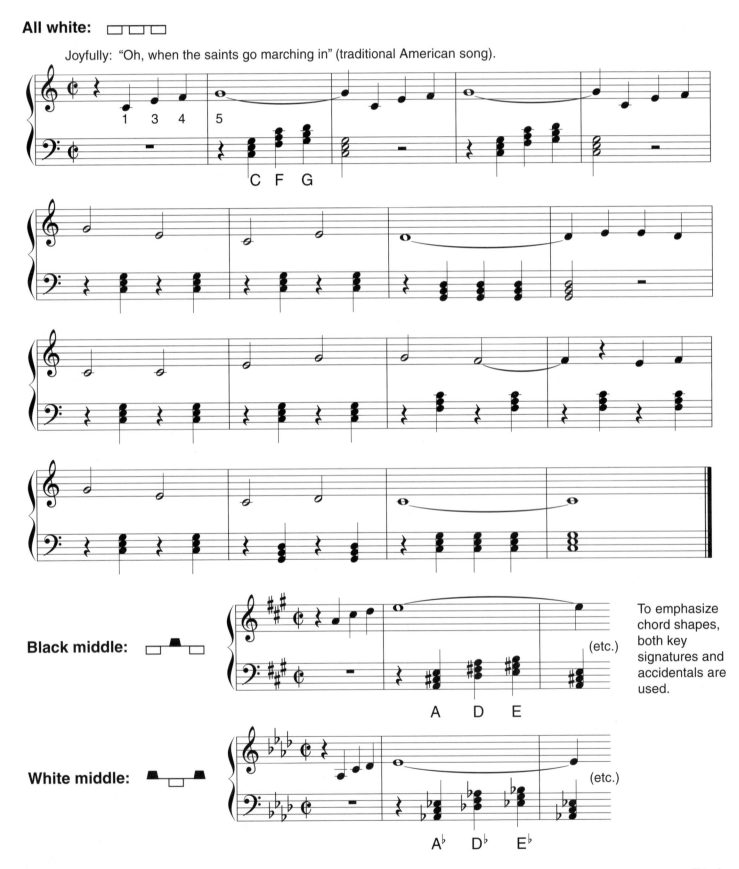

To emphasize chord shapes, both key signatures and accidentals are used.

Triads

PLAY Major Triads Using Key Signatures Instead of Accidentals

Now or later

Here is your long-range goal! Major triads on this chart are written
with key signatures, the way you will often find them in music.

After you know key signatures, come back to this page to find out
if your hands form the Lift-Out shapes automatically.

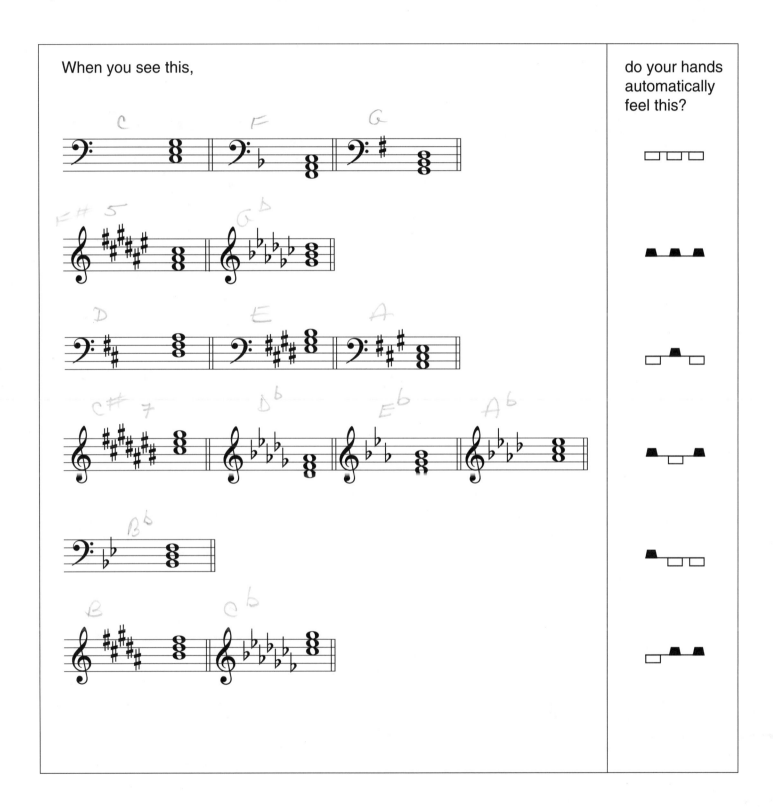

BUILD the Circle of Fifths to Learn Key Signatures for Chord Applications
Step 1. Join 5-Note Major Patterns up the Keyboard

Now or later

Play across the keyboard to play around the Circle of Fifths.

Start on the lowest **C** on the keyboard. Each new key is a fifth higher. The first tone of every scale is called the tonic.

TIP

Use your 5-Note Major Pattern map to guide you. Slide it so that you begin the next pattern on the top note of the previous pattern.

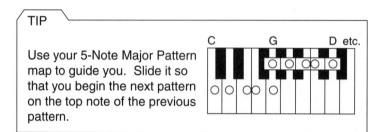

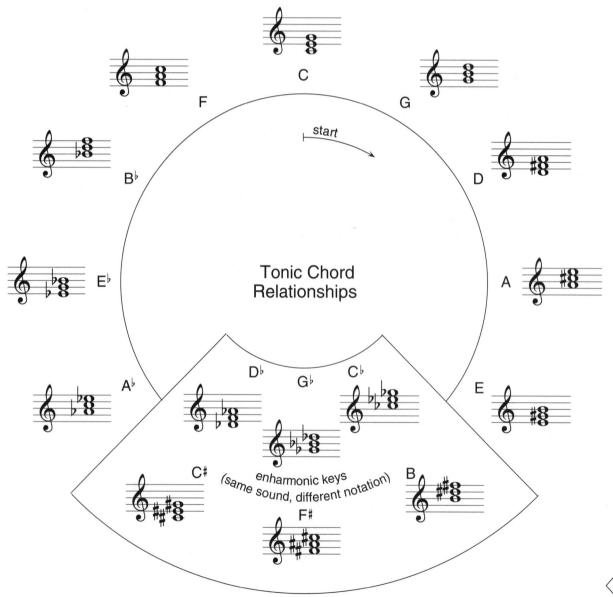

Tonic Chord Relationships

start

enharmonic keys
(same sound, different notation)

Triads

Step 1 (continued).

Now or later

When you play all the way *across* the keyboard from the lowest **C**,
you have played all the way *around* the Circle of Fifths.

Here is another way to view what you played on page 24.

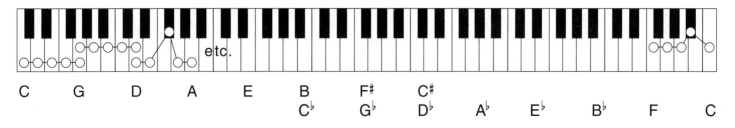

| C | G | D | A | E | B | F# | C# | | | | | | |
| | | | | | C♭ | G♭ | D♭ | A♭ | E♭ | B♭ | F | C |

On the next page, when you play across the keyboard
with overlapping 8-Note Major scales, you will have all the
sharps and flats used for key signatures under your fingers.

Turn the page and look at the key signatures on the Circle of Fifths.
Compare them to the numbers on this Circle.

Notice that the numbers are like
a clock in mirror image.

Why learn the Circle of Fifths?
It gives you a structure to understand the choice of keys and modulations in music.
Jazz musicians also use it when harmonizing melodies and improvising.

Triads

FEEL Key Signatures under Your Fingers
Step 2. Play Interlocking 8-Note Major Scales and Gather the Accidentals into Key Signatures

Now or later

Use tetrachord fingering (no thumbs) so you can feel how the scales interlock as you proceed around the Circle.

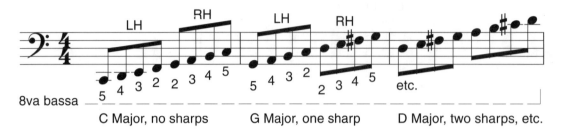

8va bassa

C Major, no sharps   G Major, one sharp   D Major, two sharps, etc.

Notice that the top tetrachord (four notes) of the first scale becomes the bottom tetrachord of the next scale.

Start with the lowest **C** on the keyboard.
Each new key is a fifth higher.

FEEL the contour of each scale.
It is the basis for the hand shape on a chord.

TIP

Use your 8-Note Major Scale Map to guide you.

7th scale degree: add the new sharp or remove the last flat

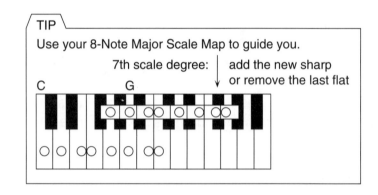

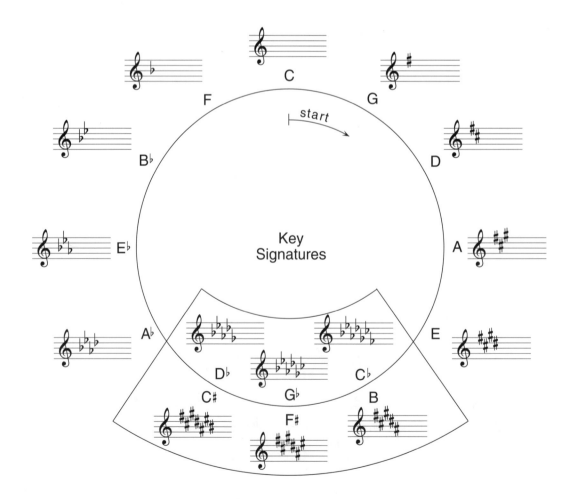

Triads

PLAY 8-Note Major Scales to See All the Sharps or Flats You Need

When you spell scales,
1. Keep the order of the musical alphabet: A B C D E F G A B C D E F G.
2. Add sharps or flats (accidentals) to keep the pattern of whole and half steps.
3. Gather the accidentals into a key signature, as shown on the opposite page.

Now or later

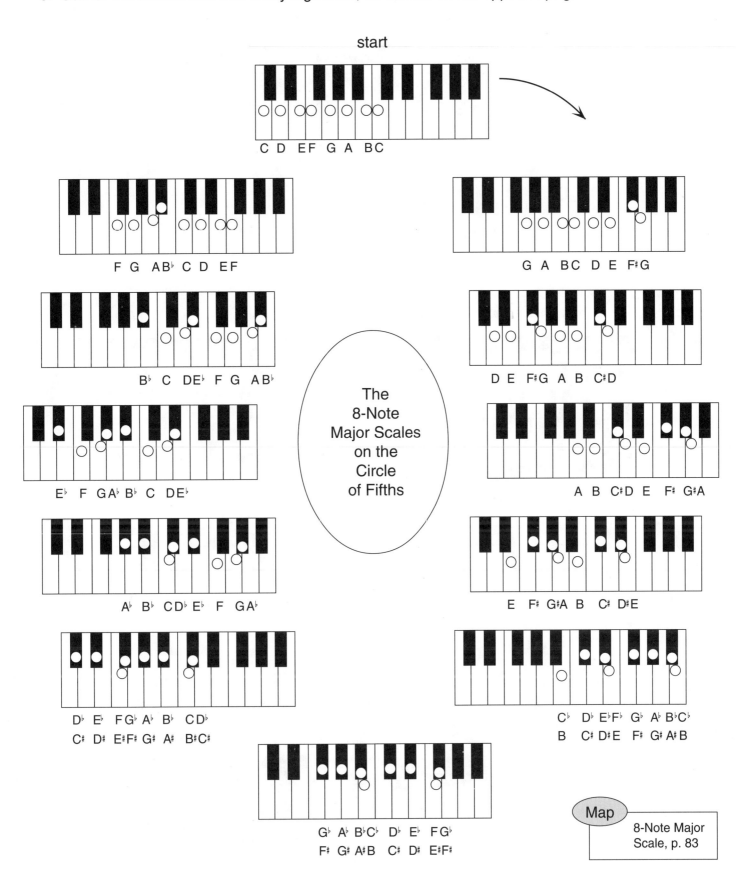

Map

8-Note Major Scale, p. 83

Triads

BUILD minor Triads from Major Triads

Want a map?

minor 5-Note Pattern, page 77

What you THINK

Lower the middle (3rd) of Major chords one half step.
On the keyboard this will feel like moving the middle of
the chord to the left, *to the closest black or white key*.

Major   (root)   ( )   (3rd)( )   (5th)

minor   (root)   ( )(3rd)   ( )   (5th)
           1   2   3   4   5

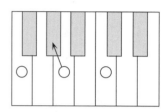

What you FEEL

F Major

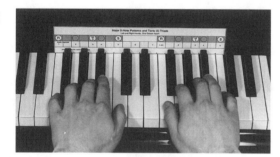

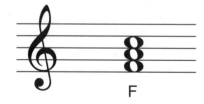

F

f minor

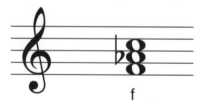

f

What you PLAY to learn it

Listen carefully to what you HEAR right here.

F Major   f minor   To emphasize the change from Major
                                  to minor, both key signature
                                  and accidentals are used.

Triads

BUILD minor Triads with Intervals

An interval is the distance between two notes.

INTERVALS

3 half steps make a minor 3rd   m3
4 half steps make a Major 3rd   M3
7 half steps make a Perfect 5th   P5

What you THINK

minor triads are the opposite of Major triads (page 17): the bottom third has 3 half steps and the top third has 4 half steps.

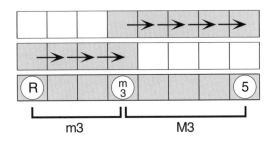

Want a map?

minor 5-Note Pattern and
One Octave Apart Patterns, page 77
Intervals, pages 52, 79

What you FEEL

f minor triad

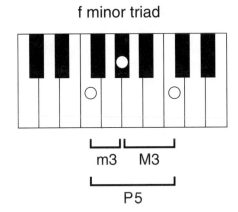

minor 3rd   Major 3rd
3 half steps   4 half steps

TIP

If you start counting half steps from zero, you will end up at the right place. Example: F G♭ G A♭ would be "zero, 1, 2, 3 half steps."

What you SEE

f minor triad

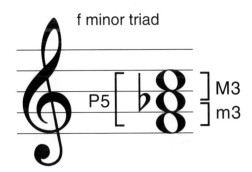

Major 3rd
4 half steps

minor 3rd
3 half steps

PLAY Parallel Major and minor Triads

Only the 3rd changes—see page 28. Listen carefully.
Play the keyboard fingerprints and read the music notation.

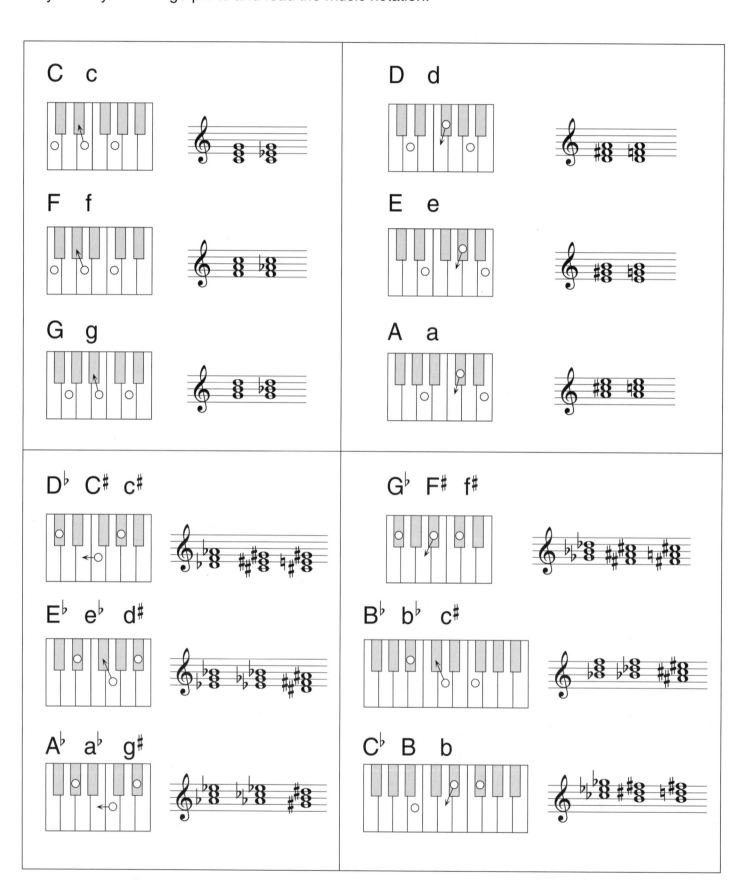

PLAY Parallel Major and minor Triads Arranged on a Ladder of Fifths

You already know all of these triads from page 30!
The ladder is another way to organize them.

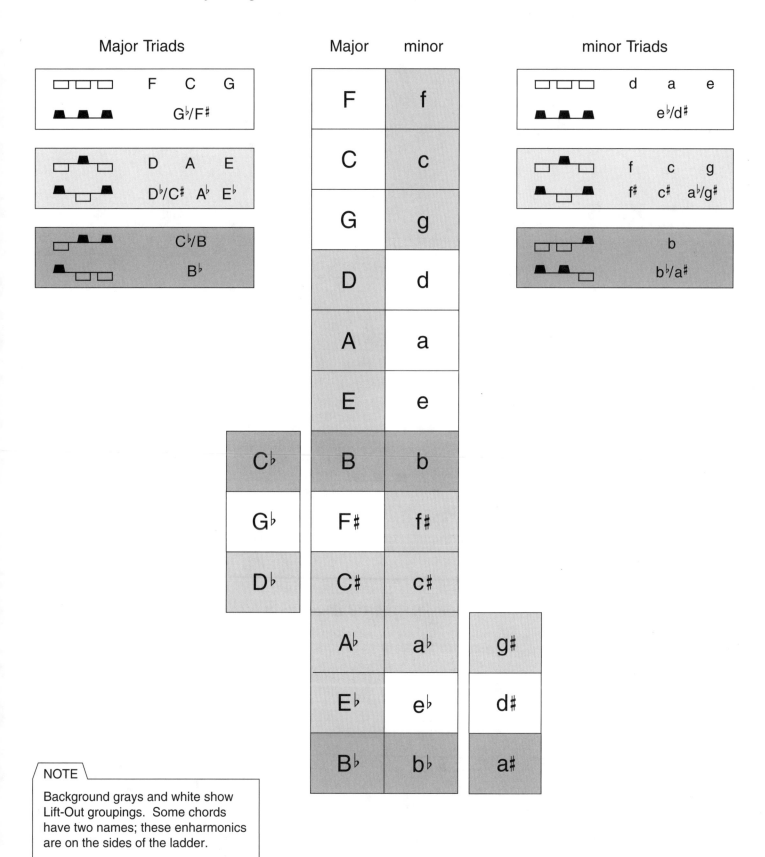

Major Triads

F C G
G♭/F#

D A E
D♭/C# A♭ E♭

C♭/B
B♭

Major minor

Major	minor
F	f
C	c
G	g
D	d
A	a
E	e
B	b
F#	f#
C#	c#
A♭	a♭
E♭	e♭
B♭	b♭

C♭
G♭
D♭

g#
d#
a#

minor Triads

d a e
e♭/d#

f c g
f# c# a♭/g#

b
b♭/a#

NOTE

Background grays and white show
Lift-Out groupings. Some chords
have two names; these enharmonics
are on the sides of the ladder.

PLAY Your Way Around the Circle of Fifths with Major Triads

You already know all these triads.
If you play clockwise, the **top** note of one chord becomes the **bottom** note of the next.
If you play counterclockwise, the **bottom** note of one chord become the **top** note of the next.

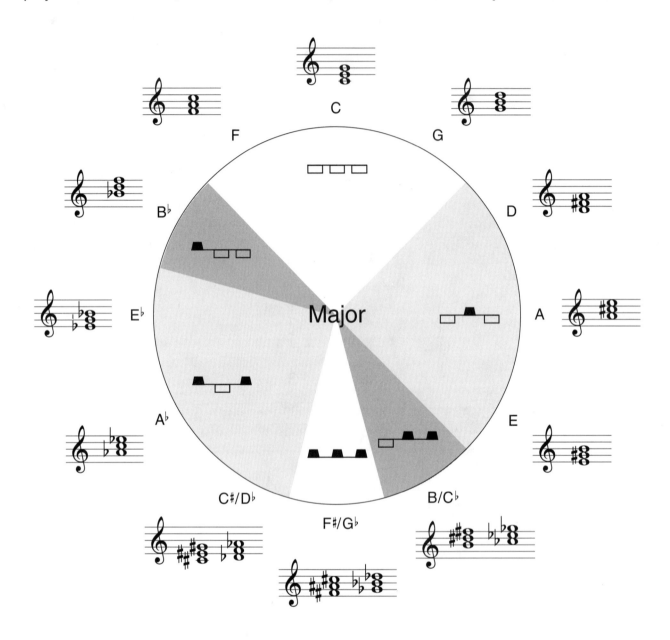

Use these rectangles:

   Play the 6 Lift-Out shapes (6 small rectangles)
   Play the 3 groups of opposites (3 large rectangles)

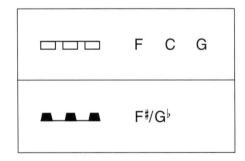
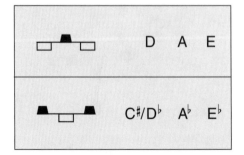
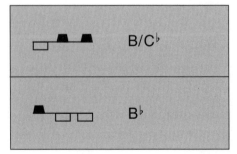

PLAY Your Way Around the Circle of Fifths with minor Triads

You already know all these triads—play the circle and the rectangles.
If you wish, write the names of the minor keys into the circle on page 26
(**a** has no accidentals, **e** has one sharp, **b** has 2 sharps, and so on).

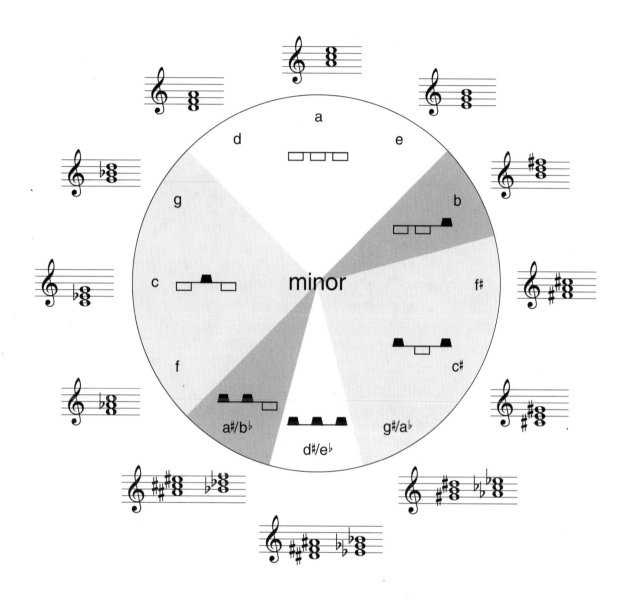

Lift-Outs are drawn with equal spacing so they work for both Major and minor.
Minor all-white and all-black Lift-Outs feel the same as Major.
Minor black-middle and white-middle Lift-Outs feel different from Major.

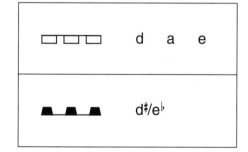
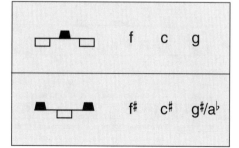
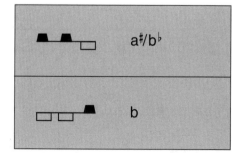

Compare **PARALLEL** Major and minor Keys

Now or later

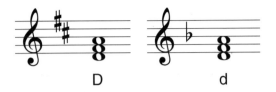

See page 31.

parallel keys

key signatures	different
tonics	same
circle of fifths location	different

parallel tonic triads

root	same
letter name	same
3^{rds}	different accidental

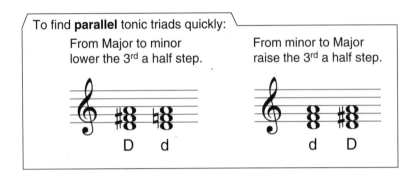

To find **parallel** tonic triads quickly:

From Major to minor
lower the 3rd a half step.

From minor to Major
raise the 3rd a half step.

"Oranges and lemons, say the bells of St. Clemens" is an old English song, harmonized on this page
in D Major/d minor and on the facing page in D Major/b minor.

After playing the minor section, you may want to go back and repeat the Major section to end
on a more cheerful note (the song was originally in Major). If you do so, you will create a three-part ABA form.

D Major

d minor

Triads

Compare **RELATIVE** Major and minor Keys

Now or later

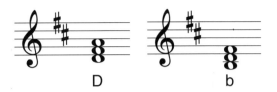

See pages 32, 33.

relative **keys**

key signatures	same
tonics	different
circle of fifths location	same

relative **tonic triads**

roots	different
letter names	different
root of Major triad is 3rd of minor triad	3rd of minor triad is root of Major triad

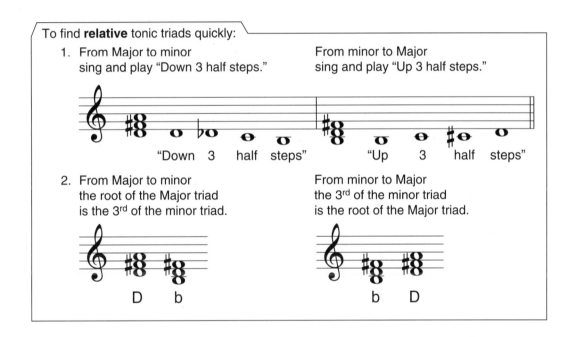

To find **relative** tonic triads quickly:

1. From Major to minor sing and play "Down 3 half steps." — From minor to Major sing and play "Up 3 half steps."

   "Down 3 half steps" — "Up 3 half steps"

2. From Major to minor the root of the Major triad is the 3rd of the minor triad. — From minor to Major the 3rd of the minor triad is the root of the Major triad.

   D b — b D

D Major

b minor

LEARN About AUGMENTED and *diminished* Triads

You have explored Major and minor triads. There are two more kinds (qualities) of triads to learn, AUGMENTED and *diminished.*

FEEL
AUGMENTED

To build an **AUGMENTED** triad, raise the 5th of a Major triad one half step:

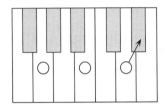

READ
AUGMENTED

AUG 5 $\left[\begin{array}{c} 8 \\ 8 \end{array}\right]$ M3 / M3

4 half steps make a Major 3rd
8 half steps make an augmented 5th

FEEL
diminished

To build a ***diminished*** triad, lower the 5th of a minor triad one half step:

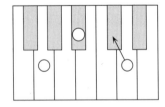

READ
diminished

dim 5 $\left[\begin{array}{c} 8 \\ 8 \end{array}\right]$ m3 / m3

3 half steps make a minor 3rd
6 half steps make a *diminished* 5th

RELATE the Four Qualities of Triads to Each Other

This map contains four layers. You can start with the Major layer and move up or down, or you may choose to start somewhere else.

HEAR four distinct sounds ("qualities"):

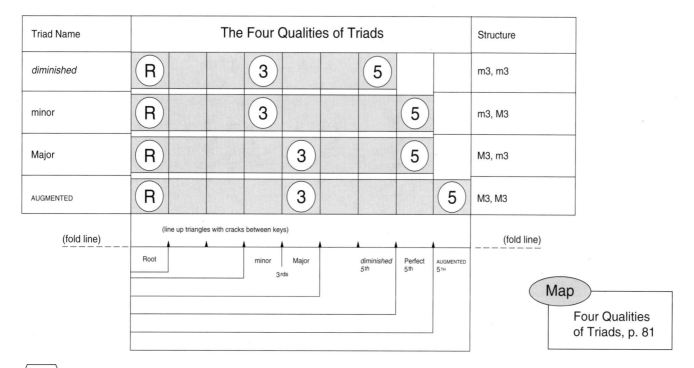

Triad Name	The Four Qualities of Triads						Structure
diminished	R		3		5		m3, m3
minor	R		3			5	m3, M3
Major	R			3		5	M3, m3
AUGMENTED	R			3			5	M3, M3

(fold line) (line up triangles with cracks between keys) (fold line)

Root   minor Major   *diminished* Perfect AUGMENTED
                         5th   5th   5TH
        3rds

Map — Four Qualities of Triads, p. 81

TIP
Play the first line right now. Play the second line (refrain) after you know the IV and V⁷ chords.

Fast and lively: "Li'l Liza Jane," Ada de Lachau.
Courtesy accidentals are omitted so you can see clearly the qualities of the triads.
The chord symbols below are explained on the next page.

G: I   IV⁶₄ I   I   IV⁶₄ I   V⁷   I

Triads

COMPARE the Four Qualities of Triads:
AUGMENTED, Major, minor, *diminished*

READ
and
LISTEN

Play the four qualities of triads, from largest to smallest, as shown below.

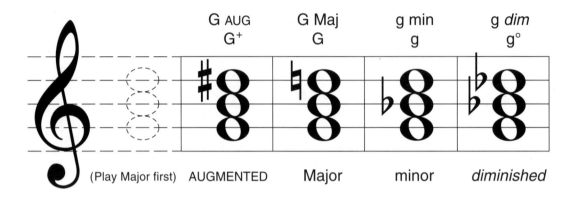

	G AUG G+	G Maj G	g min g	g *dim* g°
(Play Major first)	AUGMENTED	Major	minor	*diminished*

COMPARE

Study their intervals, shown here as blocks.

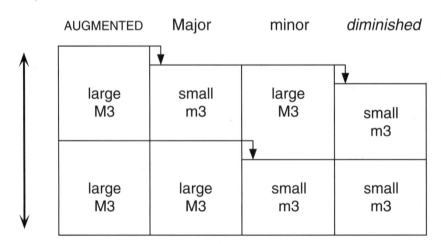

AUGMENTED	Major	minor	*diminished*
large M3	small m3	large M3	small m3
large M3	large M3	small m3	small m3

Note: A courtesy accidental is used before the G Major chord.
For clarity, courtesy accidentals are not used on the facing page.

Triads

PLAY the Four Qualities of Triads Anywhere on the Keyboard

Look at the Major column first, then play all four qualities across the row.
Select the chord or group you want.

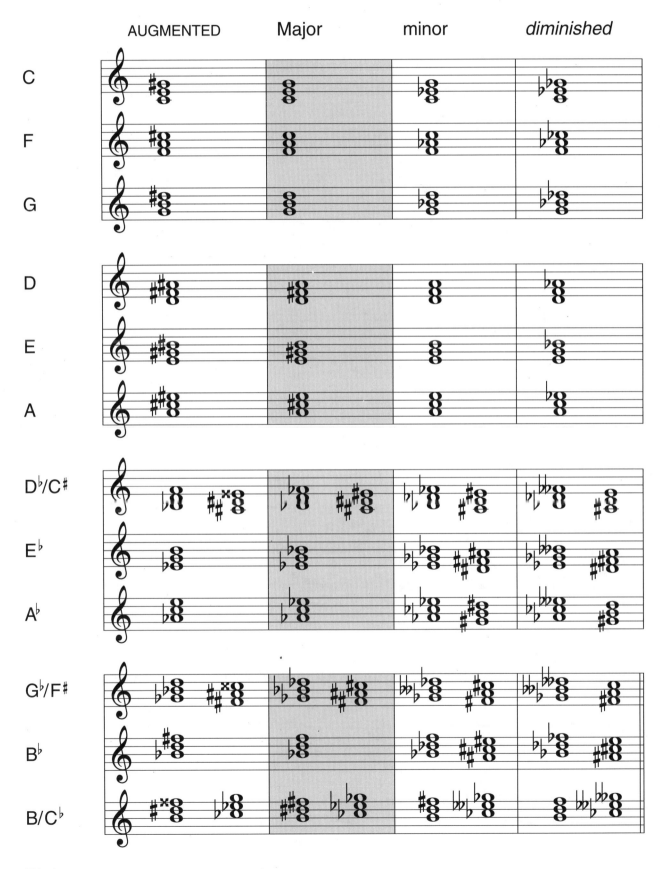

Triads

PLAY the Four Qualities of Triads in These Patterns to Put Them Securely into Your Hands

1 Try these combinations in many keys. Keep a steady rhythm.

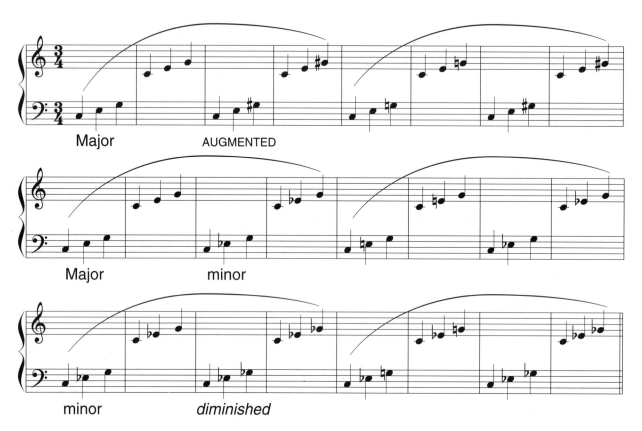

Major   AUGMENTED

Major   minor

minor   *diminished*

2 Play these five measures by chord groups: on CFG, DEA, D♭E♭A♭, G♭B♭B, non-stop.

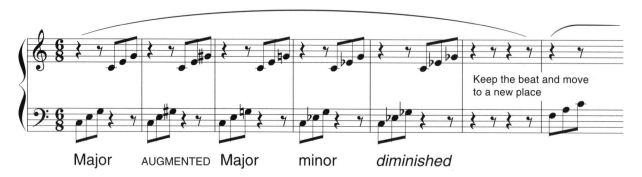

Keep the beat and move to a new place

Major   AUGMENTED   Major   minor   *diminished*

3 Think fast, but play slowly and steadily when you use this design. Then move it somewhere else.

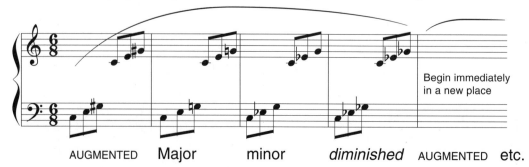

Begin immediately in a new place

AUGMENTED   Major   minor   *diminished*   AUGMENTED   etc.

Triads

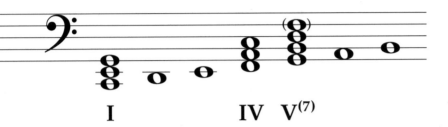

I   IV   V⁽⁷⁾

HARMONIZING

Add Root Position Chords to Melodies

- Find all the triads in any Major or minor key
  (the **7 diatonic triads**)

- Find the most frequently used chords in any key
  (the **3 primary triads**)

- Add the **Dominant Seventh** chord to your vocabulary

- Explore **accompaniment styles**

LEARN the 7 Diatonic Triads of the Major Scale

Select a key, think of its key signature, and play a triad on every scale degree, using the correct accidentals.

The example below shows the key of C Major with scale degrees (Arabic numbers) and with diatonic triads (Roman numerals).

7 Diatonic Triads

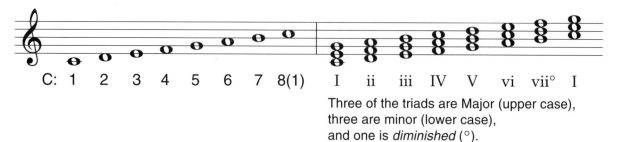

Three of the triads are Major (upper case),
three are minor (lower case),
and one is *diminished* (°).

Below is the pattern of diatonic triads that you can build in all 15 Major keys.
All of the 7 diatonic triads are useful to you for harmonizing melodies,
but I, IV and V are most frequently used.

> **NOTE**
>
> The map of the 7 diatonic triads is too tall to slide along the keyboard, so it is not presented in this book as a Movable Keyboard Map.
>
> Look at it here to understand the concept of building diatonic triads. Then just watch your hands and play a chord on each scale degree, applying the key signature of that particular scale.

Diatonic Triads of the Major Scale

SELECT the Three Most Frequently Used Chords: I   IV   and   V

Tonic   Sub-dominant   Dominant

To accompany melodies,
you need chords that will function in three ways:

- be at rest (home).
- move away (often a "lift").
- move ahead (create a sense of unrest that needs to be resolved).

Alla Marcia   "Ode to Joy" from Beethoven's Ninth Symphony.

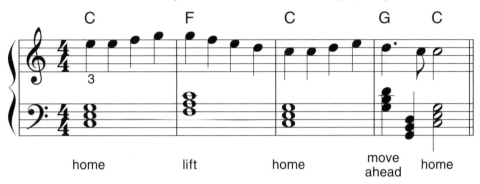

home   lift   home   move
ahead   home

3 Primary   These chords are built on scale degrees 1, 4 and 5
Triads   and are identified in Roman numerals as I, IV and V.
They are called the **3 primary triads** of the diatonic* scale.

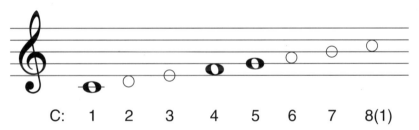

C: 1   2   3   4   5   6   7   8(1)

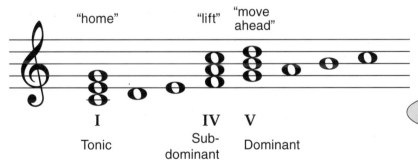

"home"   "lift"   "move
ahead"

I   IV   V

Tonic   Sub-dominant   Dominant

Want a map?

Primary Triads, page 83

This map is taken out of the complete map on page 42.

*notes that match the Major scale pattern

ADD COLOR to Your Playing with the Dominant Seventh (V^7) Chord

You have seen the Dominant (V) triad on the 5th scale degree as one of the 3 primary triads.

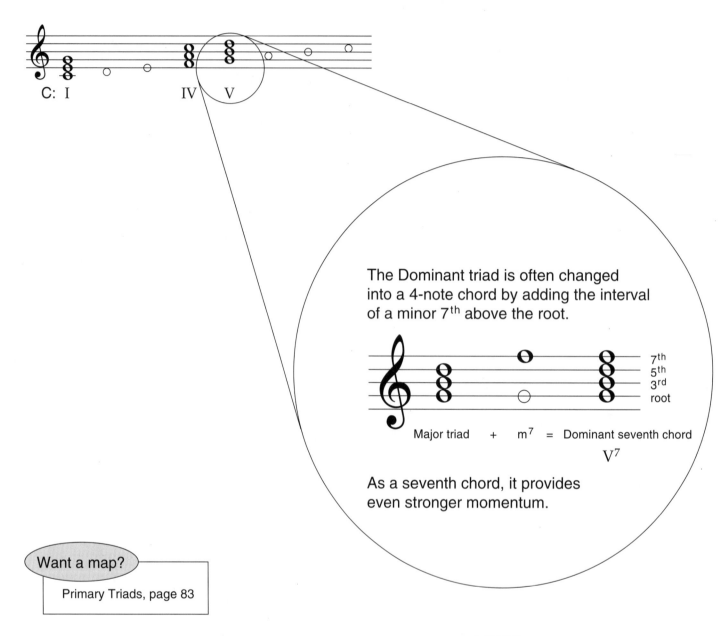

The Dominant triad is often changed into a 4-note chord by adding the interval of a minor 7th above the root.

Major triad + m^7 = Dominant seventh chord

$$V^7$$

As a seventh chord, it provides even stronger momentum.

Want a map?

Primary Triads, page 83

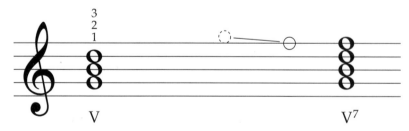

1. Play a Major triad.

2. Add the octave above and pull it down a whole step.

NOTE

The 5th of the chord is often omitted so it has the same number of notes as a triad, but you still hear it as a seventh chord.

PLAY All of the Dominant Seventh Chords

Just add a seventh to the triads you already know from page 15.
Use the Primary Triads Map, page 83. Later, after you have studied inversions,
use the Dominant Seventh Map, page 93.

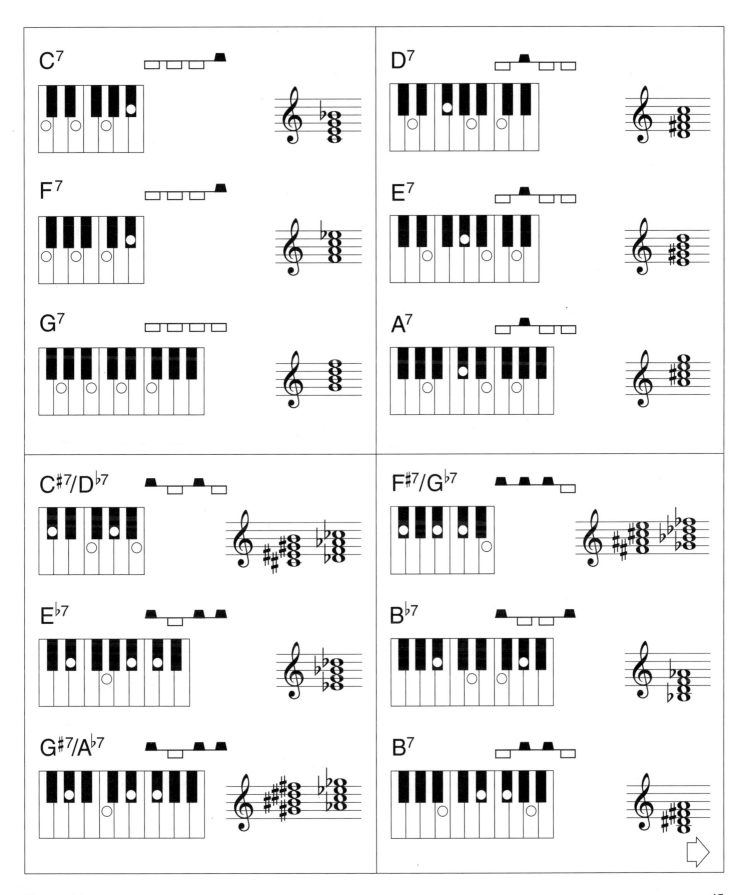

How Do You Know Which Chords Go with a Melody?

Answer: Think of the melody in scale degrees, then match the melody note to a chord containing that same scale degree.

The example below shows that in a Major key the 1st scale degree can be harmonized by the I, IV and vi chords because the 1st scale degree is one of the tones of each of those chords.

THINK of the scale degrees

Scale degrees of the Major scale

Scale degrees in the diatonic chords of the Major scale

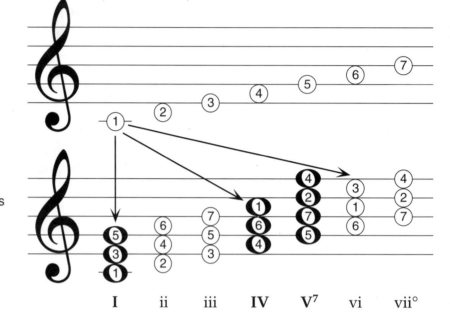

FEEL the scale degrees in your hand

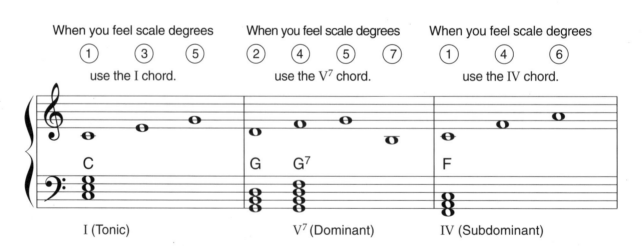

When you feel scale degrees ① ③ ⑤ use the I chord.

When you feel scale degrees ② ④ ⑤ ⑦ use the V⁷ chord.

When you feel scale degrees ① ④ ⑥ use the IV chord.

C — I (Tonic)

G — G⁷ — V⁷ (Dominant)

F — IV (Subdominant)

PREPARE YOUR HAND

Play the familiar 5-Note Major Pattern in the dotted box below.
Add the 7th scale degree below the pattern and the 6th scale degree above.
Now you have all seven scale degrees in your hand.

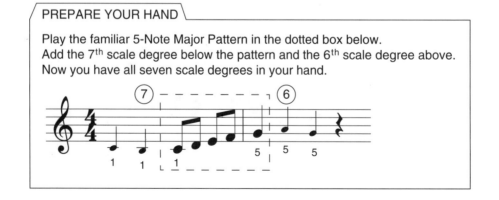

Harmonizing

An Example: Harmonizing "Frère Jacques"

1 Find your choices:

Think of the melody in scale degrees.

Make a list of the chords that match each scale degree.

I	ii	iii	I		iii	IV	V⁷		V⁷		iii	I		I	V⁷	I
vi	vii°	I	vi		I	ii	iii		iii		I	vi		vi	iii	vi
IV	V⁷	vi	IV		vi	vii°	I		I		vi	IV		IV	I	IV
						V⁷										

> **MORE CHOICES**
>
> **tempo**—A slower tempo allows for more chord changes.
> **accompaniment style**—See pages 49 and 70 for some ideas.
> **chord progression**—The order of the Roman numerals can create questions, answers, a sense of motion ahead or backward, etc.
> **non-harmonic tones**—Melody tones are chord tones or non-chord tones. In some cases a melody tone can function either way. The D in measure 1 can be harmonized with the V⁷ chord or it can be a note between the root and 3rd of the I chord, called a passing tone (PT). Because it is played quickly, the A in measure 3 is best used as an upper neighbor tone, (UNT), to the V⁷, iii, or I chord. The F in that same measure can be another PT.

2 Now explore some ways you can harmonize this melody with the Roman numerals above.

1. Begin by using the primary chords (I, IV, V, V⁷) on the strongest (first and third) beats.
2. Add primary chords on weak beats.
3. Include or substitute secondary chords (ii, iii, vi, vii°) as in the example below.

3 Here is one idea for the first four measures.
Write **your** choice of Roman numerals for the rest of the song.

C: I   V   I   I   V   vi   iii   IV   I   iii   ii   V⁷

USE Lead Sheet Notation or Roman Numerals— Shorthand Ways to Indicate Chords to Accompany a Melody

Lead Sheet Notation

LETTER NAMES of chords.

The letter name of the root, written above the melody, identifies each chord. Upper-case letters alone are used for Major chords, "7" is added to indicate Dominant seventh chords, or "m" for minor chords.

Think letter names as you play this song with chords.

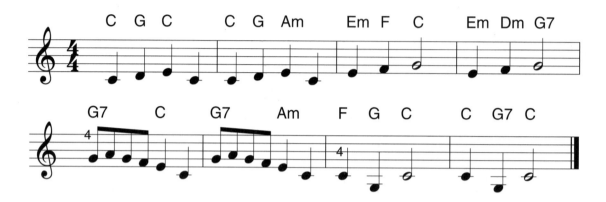

Roman Numerals

NUMBER NAMES of chords.
Play the 7 diatonic chords in C Major.

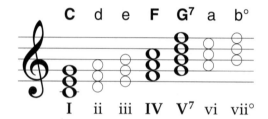

Then think Roman numerals as you play "Frère Jacques" with chords again.

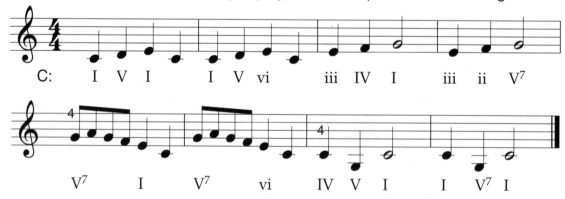

For minor chords, this book uses both lower-case letters and lead sheet notation (for example, e and Em).

CHALLENGE: Transpose

Roman numeral notation may be transferred (transposed) to any other key because it uses scale degree numbers. Try transposing "Frère Jacques" to F or G, keeping in mind the new key signature.

Harmonizing

BREAK Chords into Accompaniment Patterns

Try the patterns in the first measure only. Later play the whole song "Country Gardens."

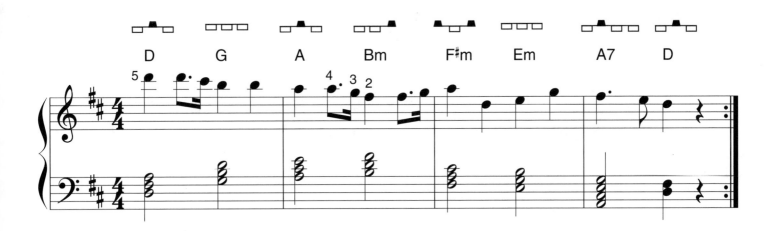

Broken chord

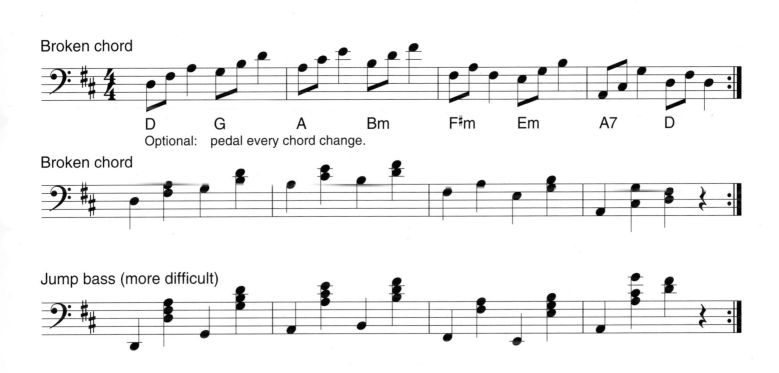

Optional: pedal every chord change.

Broken chord

Jump bass (more difficult)

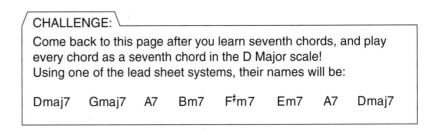

CHALLENGE:
Come back to this page after you learn seventh chords, and play every chord as a seventh chord in the D Major scale!
Using one of the lead sheet systems, their names will be:

Dmaj7   Gmaj7   A7   Bm7   F#m7   Em7   A7   Dmaj7

LOOK at the Big Picture

PLAY the 7 Diatonic Triads in Any Major Key

Every chord has a letter name ("D"), a descriptive name ("tonic"),
and a Roman numeral name ("I") that matches the scale degree number ("1").

The 3 primary triads are in bold type.

Example: D Major

Diatonic Triads								
Letter Names	**D**	e	f♯	**G**	**A**(7)	b	c♯°	**D**
Quality	Major	minor	minor	Major	Major	minor	*diminished*	Major
Scale Degrees	do 1	re 2	mi 3	fa 4	sol 5	la 6	ti 7	do 8(1)
Roman Numerals	**I**	ii	iii	**IV**	**V**(7)	vi	vii°	**I**
Triad Names	**Tonic**	super tonic	mediant	**Sub-dominant**	**Dominant**	sub-mediant	*leading tone*	**Tonic**

Diatonic triads: A **chromatic** scale employs only half steps, 12 pitches in one octave. A **diatonic** scale, such as the Major scale, employs a particular combination of 5 whole and 2 half steps, 7 pitches in every octave. Diatonic triads are built from diatonic scales.

"On Top of Old Smoky," the American folk song originally in Major mode, is written here in D Major.

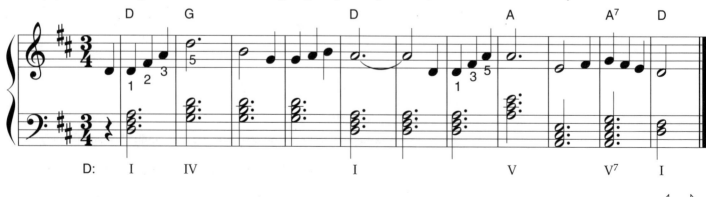

LOOK at the Big Picture

PLAY the 7 Triads in Any minor Key

Because the minor iv and Major V chords are built from it, the harmonic form of the scale is shown. The map *Intervals of the harmonic minor Scale,* page 79, also shows this scale structure.

Example: d minor

Triads	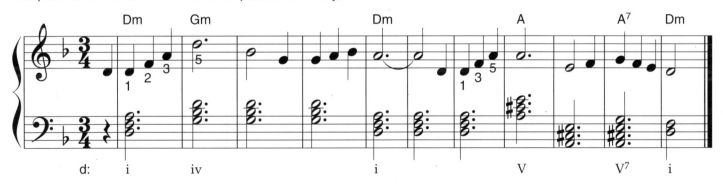							
Letter Names	**d**	e°	F⁺	**g**	A⁽⁷⁾	B♭	c♯°	**d**
Quality	minor	*diminished*	AUGMENTED	minor	Major	Major	*diminished*	minor
Scale Degrees	1	2	3	4	5	6	7	8(1)
Roman Numerals	**i**	ii°	III⁺	**iv**	V⁽⁷⁾	VI	vii°	**i**
Triad Names	**tonic**	*super-tonic*	MEDIANT	**sub-dominant**	**Dominant**	Sub-Mediant	*leading tone*	**tonic**

The III⁺ chord results from the harmonic minor scale, but is seldom used, the Major III being preferred.

Compare the sound as it would be in the parallel minor key, d minor.

Dm Gm   Dm   A   A⁷   Dm

d: i   iv   i   V   V⁷   i

LEARN Intervals of Major and harmonic minor Scales

Knowing intervals helps you play chords accurately.

MAJOR:
read and
play.

When you cut out these maps on page 79, fold them back at the 5th
if you want to use them with the 5-Note Pattern maps.

								Perfect 8th
							Major 7th	
						Major 6th		
					Perfect 5th			
				Perfect 4th				
			Major 3rd					
		Major 2nd						
Major scale degrees	1	2	3	4	5	6	7	8

Intervals of the Major Scale

Sing and
play.

To sing and play only ascending intervals (Major and perfect), stop at the double bar in the second staff.
If you also want the descending intervals (minor and perfect), keep going to the end.

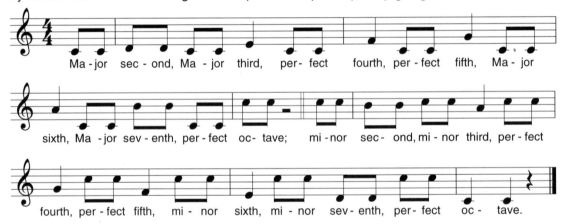

Ma - jor sec - ond, Ma - jor third, per - fect fourth, per - fect fifth, Ma - jor

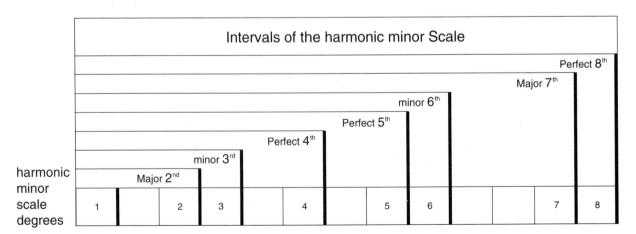

sixth, Ma - jor sev - enth, per - fect oc - tave; mi - nor sec - ond, mi - nor third, per - fect

fourth, per - fect fifth, mi - nor sixth, mi - nor sev - enth, per - fect oc - tave.

minor:
read and
play.

								Perfect 8th
							Major 7th	
						minor 6th		
					Perfect 5th			
				Perfect 4th				
			minor 3rd					
		Major 2nd						
harmonic minor scale degrees	1	2	3	4	5	6	7	8

Intervals of the harmonic minor Scale

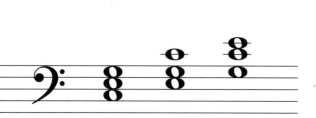

INVERSIONS

Triple the Chords You Know

STACK UP Inversions of Triads

Every triad has three positions: root position, first inversion, second inversion.

What you SEE

ON THE STAFF:

The bottom note moves to the top vertically.

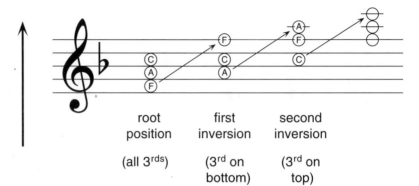

root position	first inversion	second inversion
(all 3ʳᵈˢ)	(3ʳᵈ on bottom)	(3ʳᵈ on top)

What you FEEL

ON THE KEYBOARD:

The bottom note moves to the top horizontally.

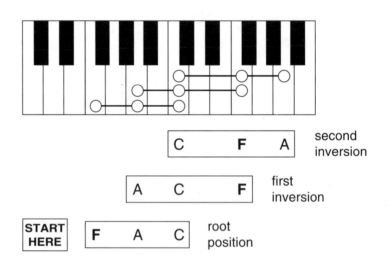

	C	F	A	second inversion
START HERE				
	A	C	F	first inversion
	F	A	C	root position

NOTE

Inversions have an interval of a fourth.

Root position triads have all thirds.

In inversions, the root is at the top of the fourth.

MOVE Through the Inversions Using the Map

To make it easier to track the root through the 3 positions, color it red on the Triad Inversions Map, page 85, and on the notes beside this photograph.

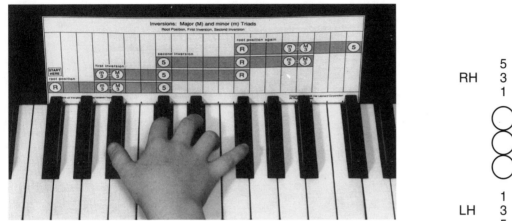

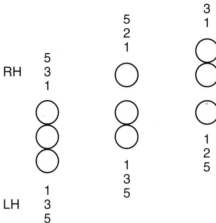

Find each position quickly with the map. Shown in F#/G♭.

Place the map with the bottom fingerprint lined up with middle C and play this 8-measure pattern. The RH fingering is always 1 3 5 except where 2 is indicated.

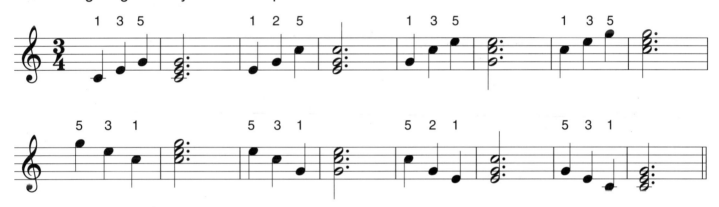

Move the map one or two octaves lower and align the bottom fingerprint with a C. The LH fingering is always 5 3 1 except where 2 is indicated.

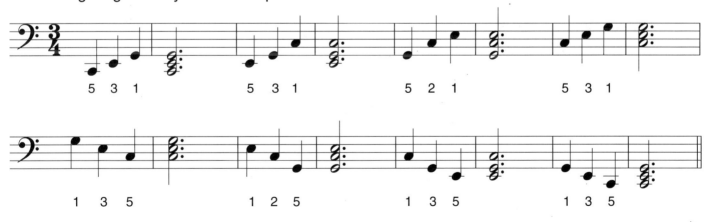

Move the map anywhere.

Inversions

PLAY All of the Major Triad Inversions

Your Inversions Map
makes it easy to check the notes.
Soon you won't need it any more.

They are arranged here as three groups of opposites.

All white or all black

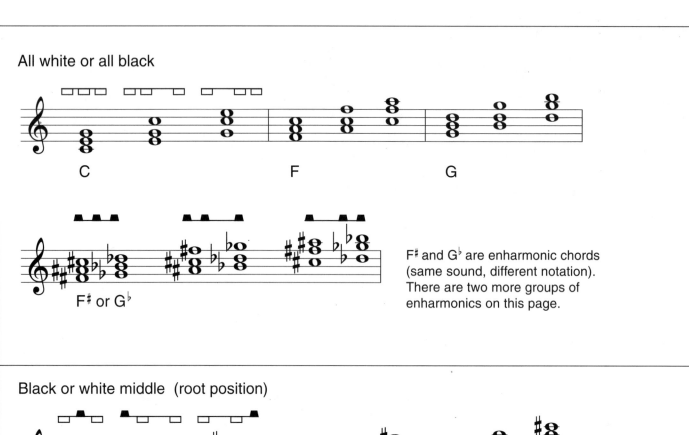

F# and G♭ are enharmonic chords
(same sound, different notation).
There are two more groups of
enharmonics on this page.

Black or white middle (root position)

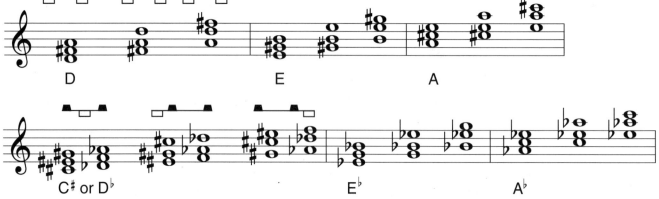

Black and white reverse (root position)

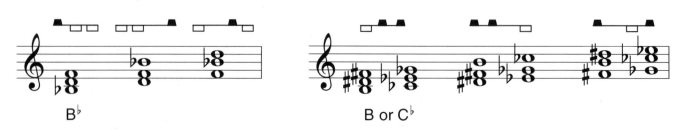

If you play each position of these chords several times,
it is easier for the hands to "remember" each shape.

Inversions

PLAY Major Triad Inversions by Just Thinking Lift-Outs

It's simple—this page gives you all the information on the facing page.

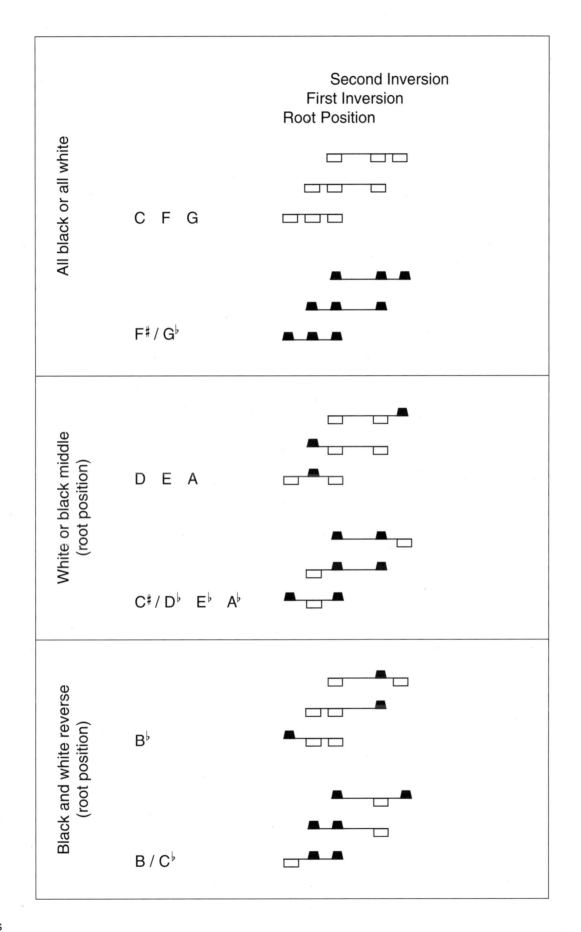

LOOK for Inversions in Pieces You Play

Use them to keep the momentum going.
Use them to add more sound.

"Du, Du, liegst mir im Herzen," a German folk song. "Set" the chords by playing through the left hand part first. There are more accompaniment styles on page 49. Notice the four-bar question and answer.

This song sounds good with or without pedal. All LH chords are played $\frac{1}{3}$ except where marked.

Put the B♭ Major chords into your hands first.

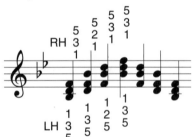

Adapted from Johann Strauss's "Blue Danube" waltz.

Put the G Major chords into your hands first.

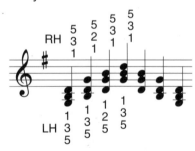

"Daisy, Daisy" (adapted from Harry Dacre). Hold the top note in the right hand for each chord. You will frequently find inversions using this texture. This is a good piece to transpose to a number of keys.

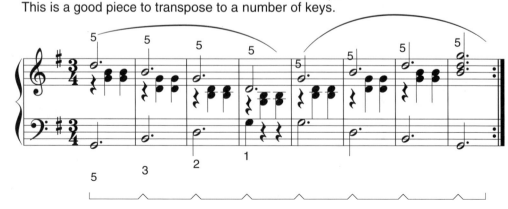

Inversions

PLAY All of the minor Triad Inversions

Your Inversions Map

makes it easy to check the notes.

They are arranged here as three groups of opposites.

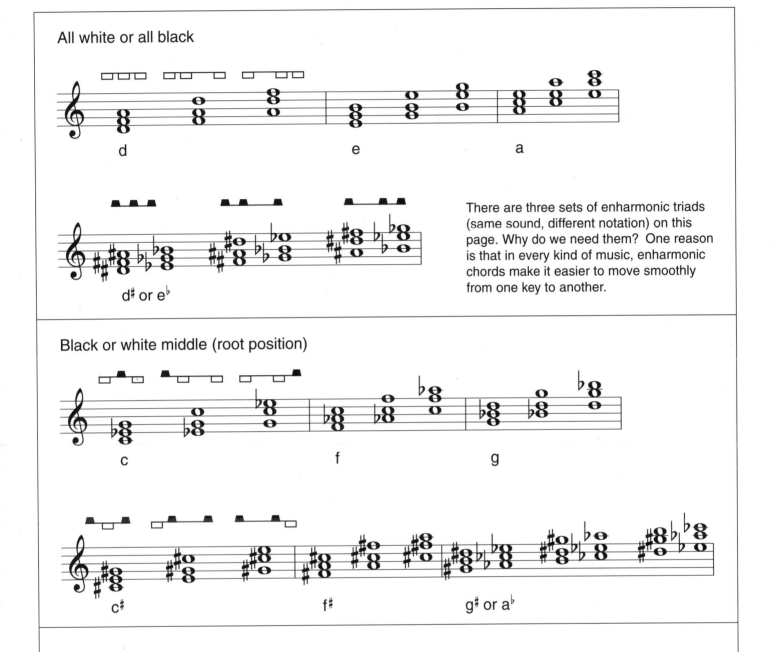

All white or all black

d   e   a

d# or e♭

There are three sets of enharmonic triads (same sound, different notation) on this page. Why do we need them? One reason is that in every kind of music, enharmonic chords make it easier to move smoothly from one key to another.

Black or white middle (root position)

c   f   g

c#   f#   g# or a♭

Black and white reverse (root position)

b♭ or a#   b

NAME Inversions by Describing the Intervals (Figured Bass)

Think bottom to top and bottom to middle.

Example: the F Major triad

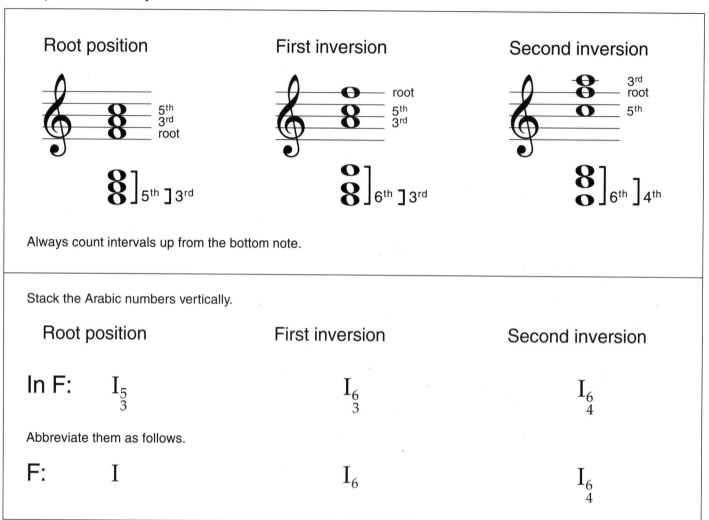

Always count intervals up from the bottom note.

Stack the Arabic numbers vertically.

	Root position	First inversion	Second inversion
In F:	I_5^3 (written $I\begin{smallmatrix}5\\3\end{smallmatrix}$)	$I\begin{smallmatrix}6\\3\end{smallmatrix}$	$I\begin{smallmatrix}6\\4\end{smallmatrix}$

Abbreviate them as follows.

F:	I	I_6	I_6^4

Excerpt from "Waltz of the Flowers" (*Nutcracker* ballet by Tchaikovsky).
First play left hand m. 3-4 a few times to get the shape of the inversions into your hand.

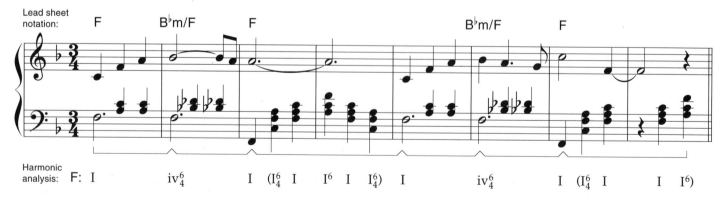

Lead sheet notation above the melody gives chord letter names at a glance.
The letter after the slash indicates the bass note. Harmonic analysis or figured bass
gives more detailed information by counting intervals up from the bass line.

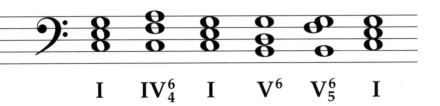

I IV^6_4 I V^6 V^6_5 I

CHORD PROGRESSIONS

Move Smoothly from Chord to Chord

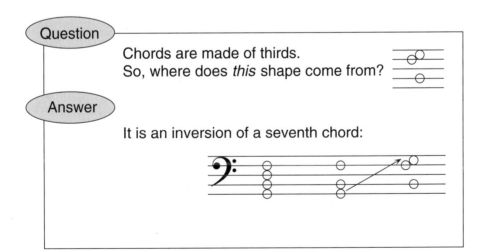

Question

Chords are made of thirds.
So, where does *this* shape come from?

Answer

It is an inversion of a seventh chord:

LEARN to Move Smoothly from Chord to Chord

What you already KNOW

You have played diatonic triads of the scale
and lifted out the primary chords I, IV, V and V^7 to harmonize melodies.

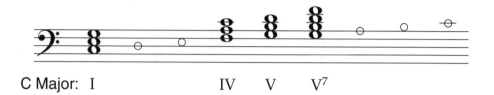

C Major: I   IV   V V^7

Your hand jumped from chord to chord
because you were using root position chords.

> **NOTE**
>
> This gave you the opportunity to explore
> the primary triads freely and play them in
> any accompaniment style as you
> harmonized melodies.

By mixing root-position chords with first- and second-inversion chords,
you can play more smoothly.

Compare these two examples of the same chord progression:

What you FEEL

All root position
(your hand jumps)

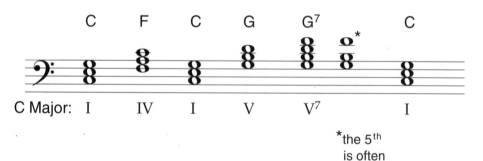

C Major: I   IV   I   V V^7 I

*the 5th
is often
omitted

What you FEEL

A mixture
(your hand barely moves)

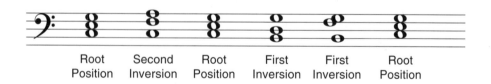

Root   Second   Root   First   First   Root
Position   Inversion   Position   Inversion   Inversion   Position

> **WHAT IS HAPPENING:**
>
> Notice that each chord shares
> a note with the next chord
> either at the bottom or the top.

Chord Progressions

DEVELOP Facility at Playing Chord Progressions Two Ways

Keyboard players need to learn chord progressions with chords in both hands
and with the root in the left hand.

> **WHY LEARN THIS?**
> Melodies often outline these chord shapes.
> Many accompaniment patterns can be
> made from them.

PRACTICE Chords in both hands

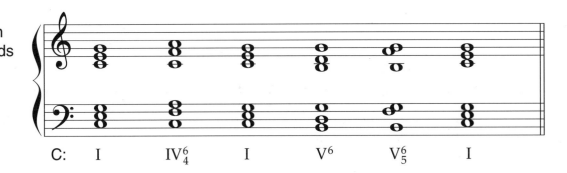

> **WHY LEARN THIS?**
> You will develop a strong sense of which note is the root.
> Intervals of 4ths and 5ths in bass lines are used in music of all styles.

PRACTICE Root in left hand

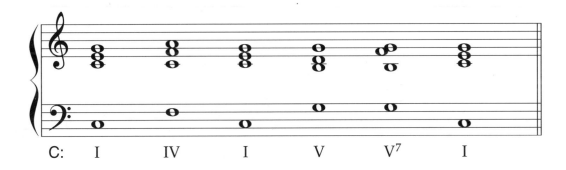

USE the maps on pages 87 and 89

Chord Name and Roman Numeral													Chord Position
		Major Chord Progression Using I and IV											
Subdominant IV		5				R			3				Second inversion IV$^6_4$
Tonic I START HERE		R			3		5						Root position I
Major scale degrees:	7	1		2		3	4	5		6		7	1	

KNOW Two Basic Chord Progressions in Major Keys

I V⁷ I   and   I IV I

PREPARE Prepare **both hands** with all the notes you will need:

Play the 5-Note Major Pattern.
Add the 7ᵗʰ scale degree below
and the 6ᵗʰ scale degree above.

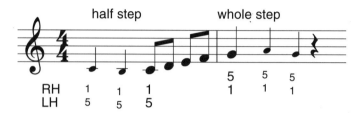

RH   1   1   1   5   5   5
LH   5   5   5   1   1   1

PLAN Select either chord progression and plan your **finger movements:**

The top stays the same.
The middle moves up a half step.
The bottom moves down a half step.

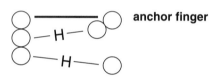

anchor finger

Tonic   Dominant
           seventh

The top moves up a whole step.
The middle moves up a half step.
The bottom stays the same.

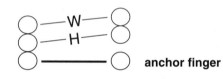

anchor finger

Tonic   Subdominant

PLAY Select the same chord progression that you played above:

C: I   V⁷   I

C: I   IV   I

Want maps?

They are on page 87
(Major Chord Progressions).

> FIGURED BASS
> Compare the left hand notes at the bottom of pages 64 and 65.
> On this page the root of each chord is the lowest note.
> On page 65 inversions of IV and V are used.
> See pages 60 and 68 for explanations of the figured bass notation.

Chord Progressions

KNOW Two Basic Chord Progressions in minor Keys

$$i \quad V_5^6 \quad i \quad \text{and} \quad i \quad iv_4^6 \quad i$$

PREPARE Prepare **both hands** with all the notes you will need:

Play the 5-Note minor Pattern.
Add the 7th scale degree below
and the 6th scale degree above.

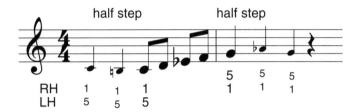

PLAN Select either chord progression and plan your **finger movements:**

The top stays the same.
The middle moves up a whole step.
The bottom moves down a half step.

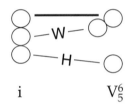

The top moves up a half step.
The middle moves up a whole step.
The bottom stays the same.

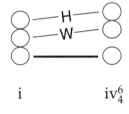

PLAY Select the same chord progression that you played above:

Want maps?

They are on page 89
(minor Chord Progressions).

CHALLENGE:
Can you play these chord progressions
in all the Major and minor keys?
Use pages 66-67.

FIND Your Major Chord Progression on This Page

hands separately
or
hands together

To play just the roots in the bass, color them red to find them easily.
You can play the complete progression or select from it (see brackets 1, 2 and 3).

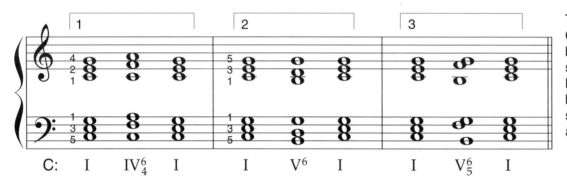

The keys of C♯ (7♯) and C♭ (7♭) are not shown because there is not space. However, the **C Major** progressions can be played with all notes sharped or flatted to achieve the same result.

C: I IV⁶₄ I   I V⁶ I   I V⁶₅ I

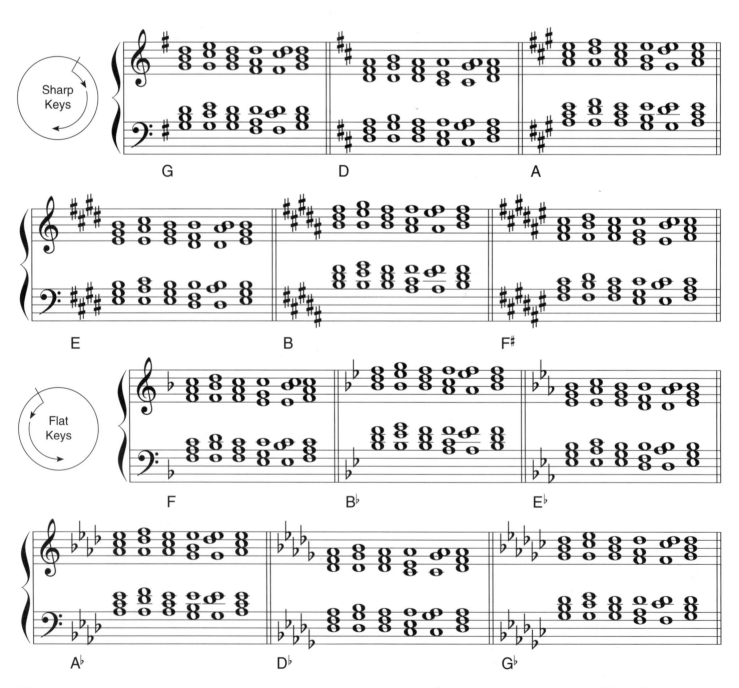

Sharp Keys

G   D   A

E   B   F♯

Flat Keys

F   B♭   E♭

A♭   D♭   G♭

Chord Progressions

FIND Your minor Chord Progression on This Page

Sometimes it is helpful to connect the chord notes with lines to show
the finger movement. Watch for the anchors.

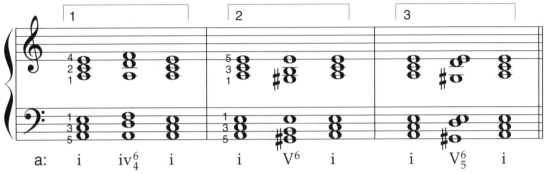

a: i iv$_4^6$ i   i V^6 i   i V$_5^6$ i

The keys of a♯ and a♭ are
not shown because there
is not space. However,
the progressions in
a minor can be played
with all notes sharped
(and 7th degree raised to
g×) or all notes flatted
(and 7th degree raised to
g♮) to achieve the same
result.

TAKE A CLOSER LOOK to See an Easy Way to Build

the Dominant Triad (V^6) and Dominant Seventh (V^6_5) First Inversions

You have seen Dominant and Dominant seventh chords in chord progressions.

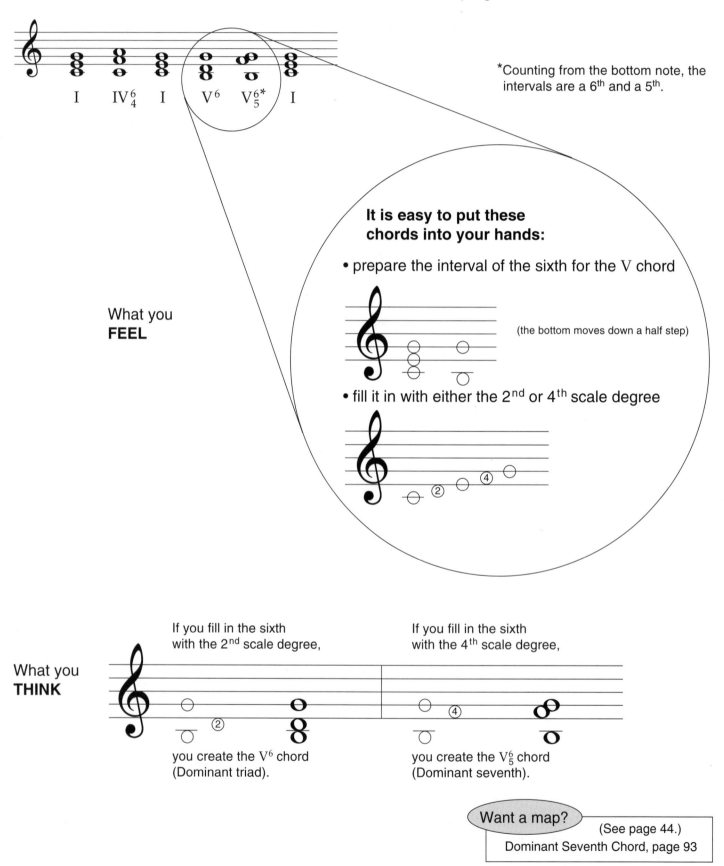

*Counting from the bottom note, the intervals are a 6th and a 5th.

It is easy to put these chords into your hands:

- prepare the interval of the sixth for the V chord

(the bottom moves down a half step)

- fill it in with either the 2nd or 4th scale degree

What you **FEEL**

What you **THINK**

If you fill in the sixth with the 2nd scale degree,

you create the V^6 chord (Dominant triad).

If you fill in the sixth with the 4th scale degree,

you create the V^6_5 chord (Dominant seventh).

Want a map?

(See page 44.)
Dominant Seventh Chord, page 93

Chord Progressions

ADD Chords to Melodies—Ease into the Next Chord Smoothly

MATCH
the scale
degrees

On page 46 when you felt these scale degrees in your right hand,

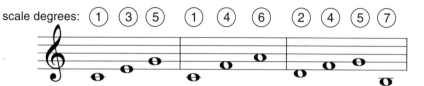

your left hand jumped to play **root position** chord progressions.

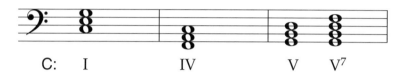

Now your hand can go smoothly to these chords by using **inversions.**

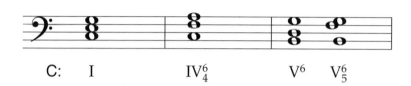

FEEL
the chords
outlined
by the
melody

If you have put the chord progressions on pages 66-67 into your hands, often your right hand will automatically "recognize" that the melody is outlining the chord your left hand needs for the accompaniment pattern. (Block the chords with both hands before playing the song.)

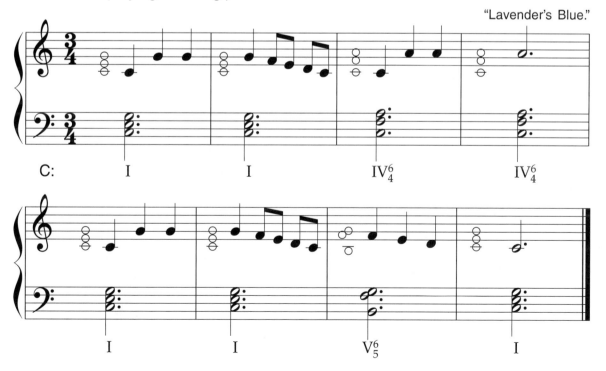

"Lavender's Blue."

ACCOMPANIMENT PATTERNS Using I, IV$_4^6$ and V$_5^6$ Chords

Try harmonizing a familiar melody with broken chords, waltz bass, and Alberti bass.
In lead sheet notation, the letter after the slash indicates the lowest note.

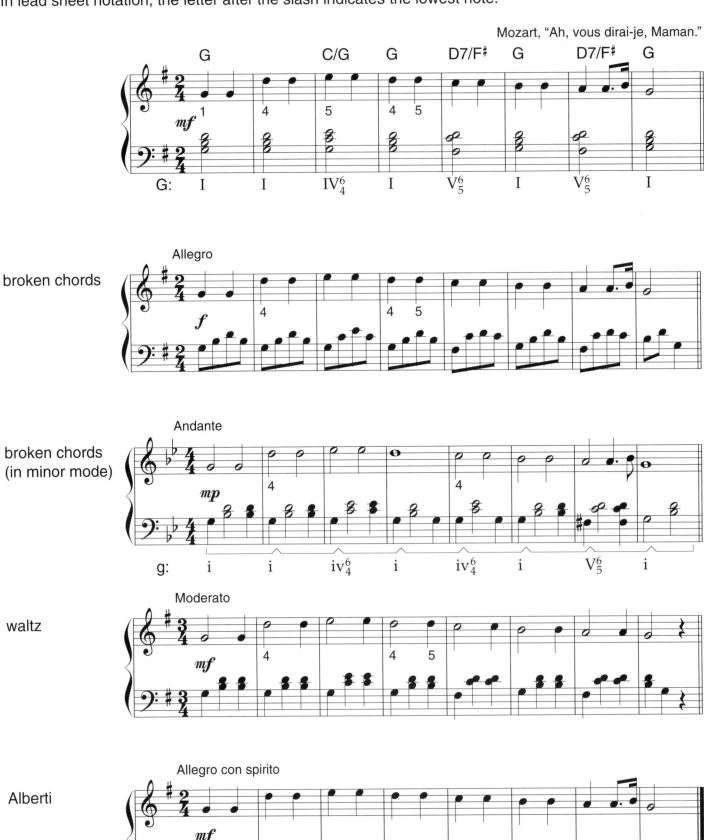

Chord Progressions

SEVENTH CHORDS

Use them to accompany a song or improvise

- 5 Qualities of seventh chords

- Dominant seventh inversions

- Jazz nomenclature

"…Crying cockles and mussels, alive, alive-o…" from Dublin.
Play it again an octave higher for a more delicate sound.

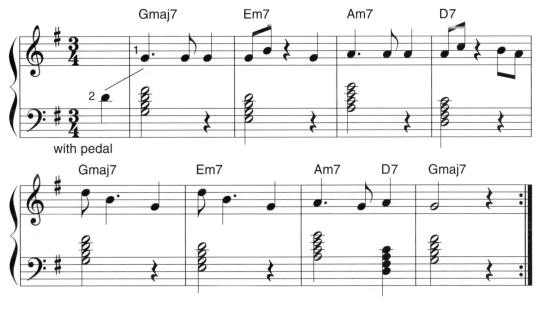

LEARN the Five Qualities of Seventh Chords

A chord with four notes is called a SEVENTH CHORD. In music notation, a root position seventh chord has four notes that touch. It can be written on lines or in spaces.

Seventh chord letter names

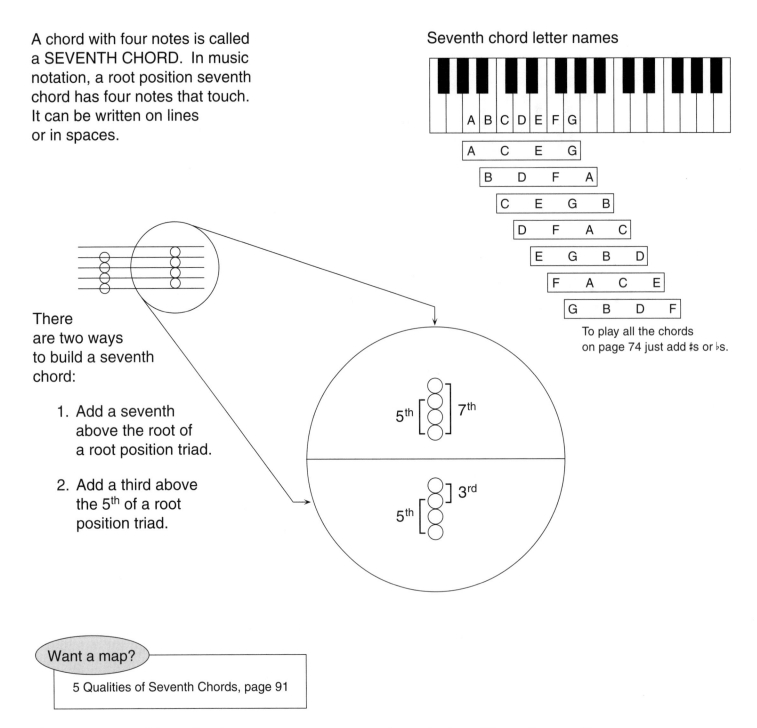

To play all the chords on page 74 just add ♯s or ♭s.

There are two ways to build a seventh chord:

1. Add a seventh above the root of a root position triad.

2. Add a third above the 5th of a root position triad.

Want a map?

5 Qualities of Seventh Chords, page 91

There are 5 qualities (sizes) of seventh chords, as shown below. Name the quality of the triad first, then the interval of the seventh (MM = Major triad, Major 7th).

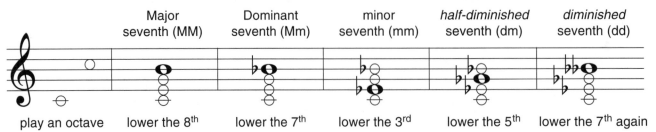

	Major seventh (MM)	Dominant seventh (Mm)	minor seventh (mm)	*half-diminished seventh (dm)*	*diminished seventh (dd)*
play an octave	lower the 8th	lower the 7th	lower the 3rd	lower the 5th	lower the 7th again

Seventh Chords

PLAY the Five Qualities of Seventh Chords

Let the map guide you through the series of seventh chords shown on page 72.

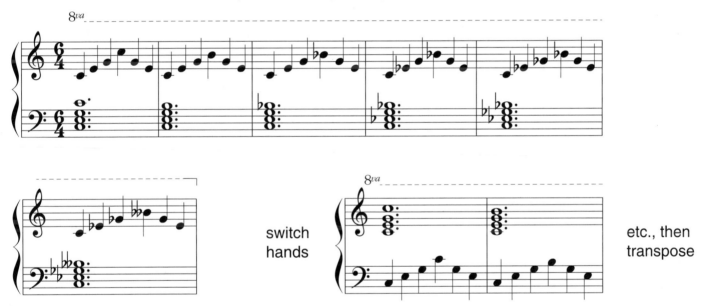

Chord Name	Five Qualities of Seventh Chords						7ths diminished	7ths minor	7ths Major	8th Octave	Jazz Symbols
diminished seventh	R		3		5		7			◯	°7
half-diminished seventh	R		3		5			7		◯	ø7
minor seventh	R		3			5		7		◯	m7
Dominant seventh	R			3		5		7		◯	7 (Dominant)
Major seventh	R			3		5			7	◯	M7

↑ START HERE   (line up triangles with cracks between keys)

Listen to the different sounds as you increase your keyboard facility.

switch hands

etc., then transpose

Dominant seventh inversions:

The map on page 91 compares the five qualities with each other in root position.
On page 93 the map shows the Dominant seventh in all positions because it is used most often.

C triad and Dominant seventh inversions are compared here. A 4-note chord has four positions. A 3-note chord has three positions, as shown on page 60.

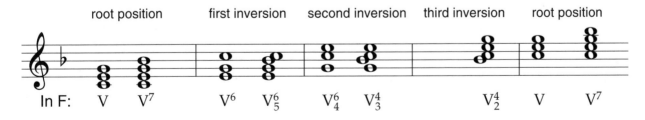

root position | first inversion | second inversion | third inversion | root position

In F: V   V⁷   V⁶   V⁶₅   V⁶₄   V⁴₃   V⁴₂   V   V⁷

FIND and PLAY the Seventh Chord You Want

Use the Five Qualities of Seventh Chords Map (page 91) to find the notes and this page to understand the spelling. All diminished seventh chords are spelled here from the root. In cases where the "correct" spelling is hard to read, one of the enharmonic spellings is also given.

	Major seventh	Dominant seventh	minor seventh	*half-dim.* seventh	*diminished* seventh

READ Lead Sheet Notation in Fake Books, Popular Music and Jazz

Triads and seventh chords are among the sounds used to accompany popular music.
This page shows a few basic chords and symbols. There are many more.

In lead sheet notation a chord's letter name is written above a melody note or rest.
Upper-case letters are used for Major chords and "m" is added to indicate a minor chord.

This example uses Dominant seventh chords, shown by "7," and a triad.

"St. Louis Blues," W. C. Handy.

Here is a summary of the five qualities of seventh chords, shown
with lead sheet labels. To build a seventh chord, think of the triad first.
The five qualities are based on Major, minor and *diminished* triads.

There are many different ways to write lead sheet symbols; two are shown here.

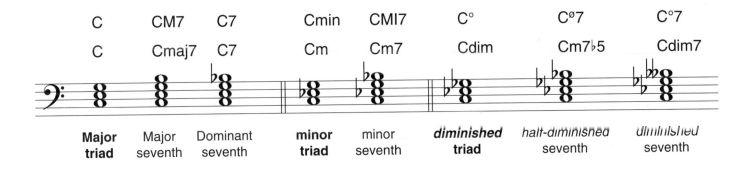

C	CM7	C7	Cmin	CMI7	C°	C°7	C°7
C	Cmaj7	C7	Cm	Cm7	Cdim	Cm7♭5	Cdim7
Major triad	Major seventh	Dominant seventh	**minor triad**	minor seventh	**diminished triad**	half-diminished seventh	diminished seventh

WHAT DOES A LETTER AFTER A SLASH MEAN?
If a chord label appears with a slash, the letter
after the slash shows which note is in the bass.

ADDED SIXTHS
These chords, with a sixth added
above the root of a Major or minor triad,
are often used in jazz improvisation and
lead sheet harmonization. Here are examples:

FIND IT FAST (A list of the most important explanation or summary pages)

Concept	Choices		Go to
accompaniment patterns			49, 70
add chords to melodies (harmonize)			46-47, 69
chord progressions			64-65, 66-67
chords	AUGMENTED		36, 39
	diatonic triads		42, 50-51
	diminished		36, 39
	dominant seventh		44-45, 68
	jazz notation		75
	Major		15
	minor		30
	primary triads		43
	seventh		72, 74
circle of fifths	build and play using 5-note patterns		24
		using 8-note scales	26
	with tonic chords		24, 32-33
		Major key signatures	26
figured bass			48, 60, 68
half/whole steps	on keyboard		10
	on maps		5
intervals	Major	scale	52
		triad	17
	minor	scale	52
		triad	29
inversions	triads,	Major	56, 57
		minor	59
	seventh chords		61, 68, 73
key signatures	Major keys		26
	parallel relationship		34
	relative relationship		35
lead sheet notation			48, 75
scale pattern	5-note	Major	13
		minor	28
	8-note	Major	10-11, 27
		minor (harmonic)	51, 52
spell	chords		16
	Major scale		27

Cut-out Page: Movable Keyboard Maps
(Slide either Map to begin on any black or white key)

Intervals of the harmonic minor Scale

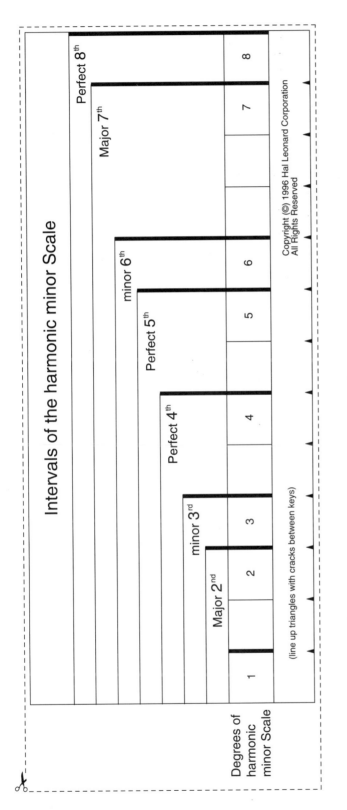

Intervals of the Major Scale

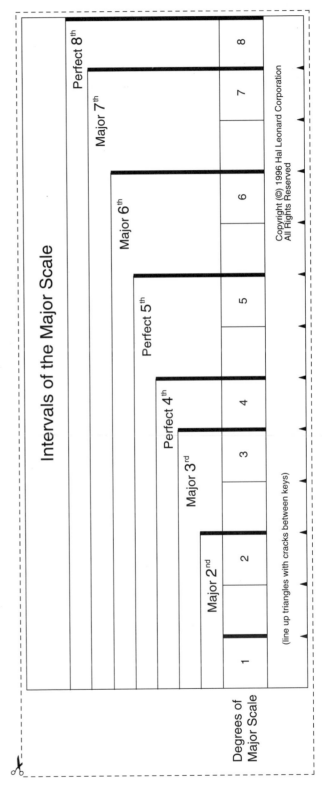

Cut-out Page: Movable Keyboard Map
(Slide the Map to begin on any black or white key)

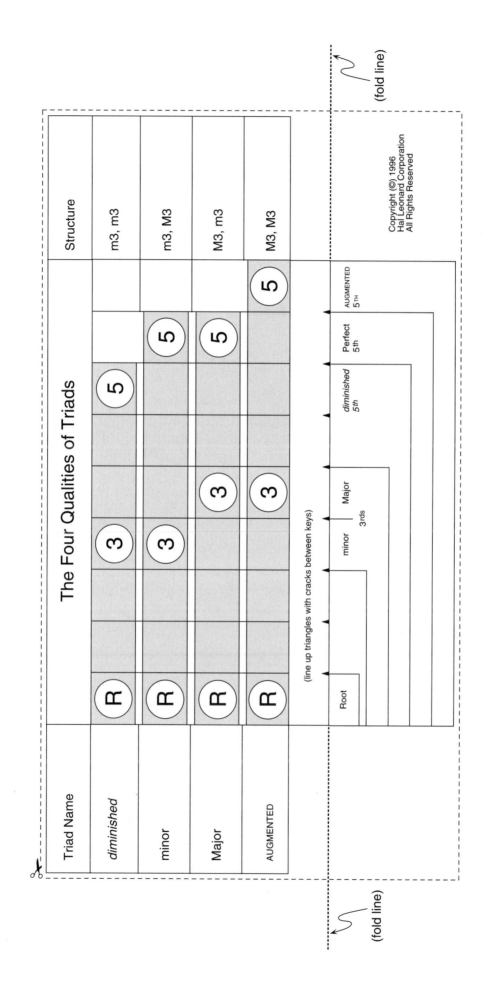

The Four Qualities of Triads

Triad Name						Structure
diminished	R	3	5			m3, m3
minor	R	3		5		m3, M3
Major	R		3	5		M3, m3
AUGMENTED	R		3		5	M3, M3

(line up triangles with cracks between keys)

Root — minor | Major — *diminished* 5th — Perfect 5th — AUGMENTED 5TH

3rds

(fold line)

(fold line)

Cut-out Page: Movable Keyboard Maps
(Slide either Map to begin on any black or white key)

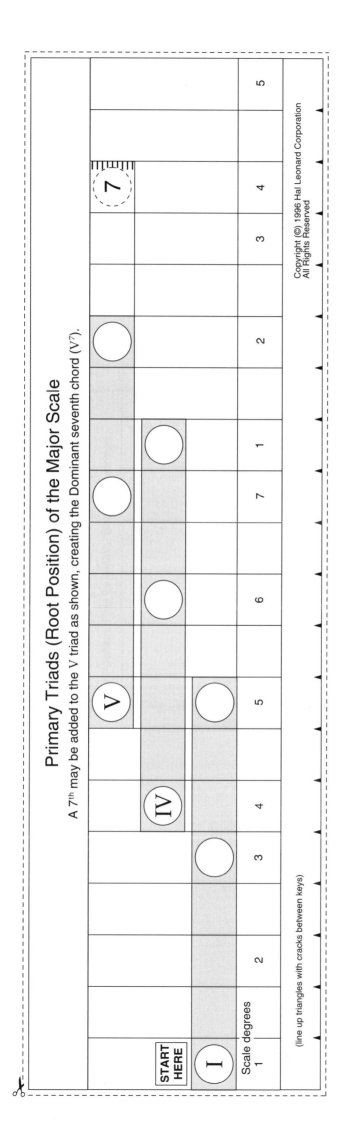

Primary Triads (Root Position) of the Major Scale

A 7th may be added to the V triad as shown, creating the Dominant seventh chord (V⁷).

(line up triangles with cracks between keys)

Cut-out Page: Movable Keyboard Map

(Slide the Map to begin on any black or white key)

Inversions: Major (M) and minor (m) Triads

Root Position, First Inversion, Second Inversion

root position again

second inversion

first inversion

START HERE
root position

(line up triangles with cracks between keys)

R · M/3 · m/3 · 5 · R · 5 · R

Cut-out Page: Movable Keyboard Maps
(Slide either Map to begin on any black or white key)

Major Chord Progression Using I and IV

Chord Name and Roman Numeral	Chord Position	Major scale degrees
Subdominant IV	Second inversion IV$_4^6$	(circles: 5, R, 3)
Tonic I — START HERE	Root position I	(circles: R, 3, 5)
		7 1 2 3 4 5 6 7 1

(line up triangles with cracks between keys)

Major Chord Progression Using I, V^7 and V

Chord Name and Roman Numeral	Chord Position	Major scale degrees
Dominant triad V	First inversion V^6	(circles: 3, 5, R)
Dominant seventh V^7	First inversion V$_5^6$	(circles: 3, 7, R)
Tonic I — START HERE	Root position I	(circles: R, 3, 5)
		7 1 2 3 4 5 6 7 1

(line up triangles with cracks between keys)

Cut-out Page: Movable Keyboard Maps

(Slide either Map to begin on any black or white key)

minor Chord Progression Using i and iv

Chord Position

second inversion	iv$^6_4$	
root position	i	

Chord degrees: R 5 3 / R 3 5 ... 7 1 2 3 4 5 6 7 1

Chord Name and Roman Numeral

subdominant	iv
Tonic	i — START HERE

harmonic minor scale degrees: 7 1 2 3 4 5 6 7 1

(line up triangles with cracks between keys)

minor Chord Progression Using i, V^7 and V

Chord Position

First inversion	V^6	
First inversion	V$^6_5$	
Root position	i	

Chord degrees: 3 R 5 / 3 R 7 / R 5 3 ... 7 1 2 3 4 5 6 7 1

Chord Name and Roman Numeral

Dominant triad	V
Dominant seventh	V^7
tonic	i — START HERE

harmonic minor scale degrees: 7 1 2 3 4 5 6 7 1

(line up triangles with cracks between keys)

Cut-out Page: Movable Keyboard Map
(Slide the Map to begin on any black or white key)

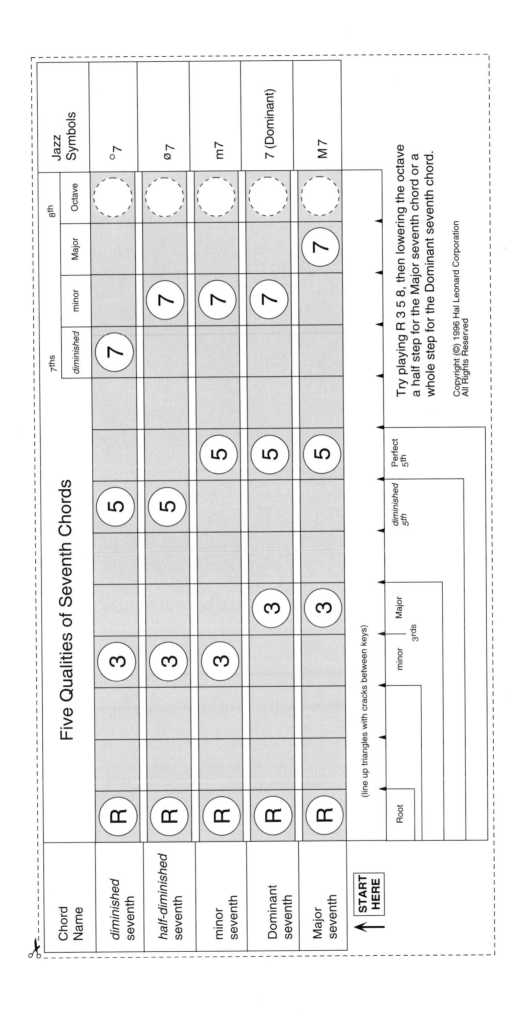

Five Qualities of Seventh Chords

Chord Name											7ths			8th	Jazz Symbols
											diminished	minor	Major	Octave	
diminished seventh	R		3			5			7						◯	°7
half-diminished seventh	R		3			5				7					◯	Ø7
minor seventh	R		3				5			7					◯	m7
Dominant seventh	R		3	3			5			7					◯	7 (Dominant)
Major seventh	R			3			5				7				◯	M7

(line up triangles with cracks between keys)

Root		minor	Major		*diminished* 5th	Perfect 5th
			3rds			

Try playing R 3 5 8, then lowering the octave a half step for the Major seventh chord or a whole step for the Dominant seventh chord.

START HERE

Cut-out Page: Movable Keyboard Map
(Slide the Map to begin on any black or white key)

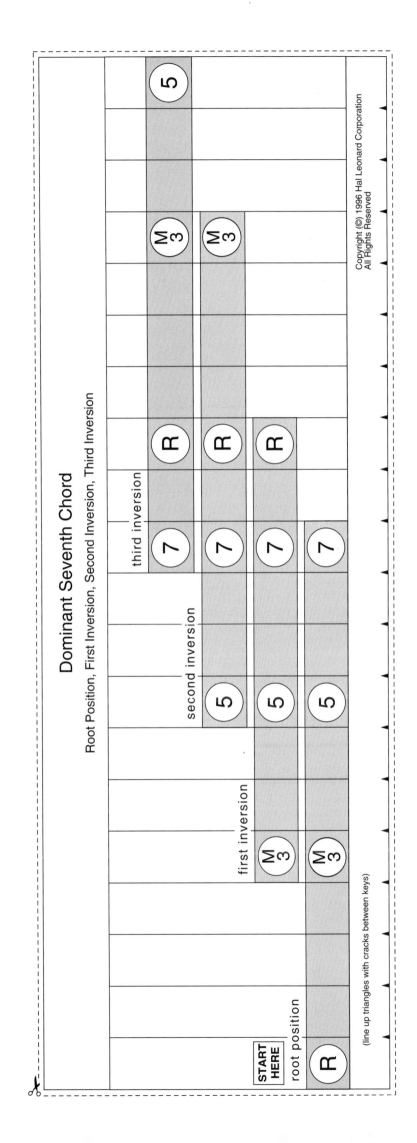

Dominant Seventh Chord
Root Position, First Inversion, Second Inversion, Third Inversion